The Spokesman

The Suicide Bombers
Edited by Ken Coates

Published by Spokesman for the
Bertrand Russell Peace Foundation

Spokesman 87   2005

CONTENTS

Editorial	3	
Joy Shall Be in Heaven ...	7	*Robert S. McNamara*
The Final Abyss?	15	*Admiral of the Fleet The Earl Mountbatten of Burma*
The Nuclear Future?	19	*Zia Mian*
Three Poems	24	*Kurt Vonnegut*
Albert Einstein	25	*Bertrand Russell*
Mesopotamia 1917	27	*Rudyard Kipling*
World Tribunal on Iraq	28	*John Berger*
The Age of Irony	29	*Arundhati Roy*
How the UN Failed Iraq	32	*Hans von Sponeck*
Unfinished Business for the Peace Movement	37	*Ken Coates*
Mr Blair's Africa	45	*Michael Barratt Brown*
Ron Todd 1927 – 2005	57	
Dossier	61	Force Cuts in Iraq? Is Britain's Nuclear Arsenal to Be Replaced? Questions for President Bush US Restarts Plutonium 238 Production 'Outsourcing' Torture
Reviews	69	*Ken Coates, Tony Simpson David Burnett, Zia Mian David Gee, Ken Fleet*

Subscriptions
Institutions £30.00/€60/$60
Individuals £20.00 (UK)
£25.00 (ex UK)
€40/$40

Back issues available on request

A CIP catalogue record for this book is available from the British Library

Published by the
Bertrand Russell Peace
Foundation Ltd.,
Russell House
Bulwell Lane
Nottingham NG6 0BT
England
Tel. 0115 9784504
email:
elfeuro@compuserve.com
www.spokesmanbooks.com
www.russfound.org

Editorial Board:
Michael Barratt Brown
Ken Coates
John Daniels
Ken Fleet
Stuart Holland
Tony Simpson

Printed by the Russell Press Ltd., Nottingham, UK
ISBN 0 85124 713 X

Bakers, Food & Allied Workers Union

*Suuporting workers in struggle
Wherever they may be.*

Joe Marino   General Secretary
Ronnie Draper President
Jackie Mander Vice President

Stanborough House,
Great North Road,
Stanborough,
Welwyn Garden City,
Hertfordshire. AL8 7TA
Phone 01707 260150& 01707 259450
www.bfawu.org

Editorial
The Suicide Bombers

ONGOING TWO MINUTES SILENCE - BAGHDAD

It was not only the war on Iraq which came to London when the London underground was bombed, and that bus was destroyed in Tavistock Square. Of course a large, probably preponderant part of the British Muslim population is deeply disturbed by the wanton destruction in Mesopotamia. Falluja is a word which still makes many British politicians look for their glossaries: but most British Muslims are likely to know what it means. But it is not clear whether those who planted these bombs were motivated by outraged solidarity, or by what they had come to see as the profanation of their faith. Whatever drove them, these young people were not the only causal influences in the tragedy of which they were a part.

The London bombs went off at the climax of the G8 summit meeting in Gleneagles. Hyped round the moon and back by Bob Geldof and Bono, this momentarily raised some expectations about the relief of poverty in Africa, and the counter measures necessary to slow global warming. But it seems only too true that the cynics were largely right, and that poverty will continue to write new pages of history for some considerable time, if the intensified global warming allows. Those who cried out at previous summits, that another world is possible, had clearly been targeted by the spin-doctors, with the prodigious pop festivals, and the personal appearance of Gordon Brown among the banner carriers. However, the later sound of damp squibs at Gleneagles was completely blanked out by the explosions at Aldgate, Edgware Road, King's Cross, and Tavistock Square.

Four young British Muslims have been identified as the suicide bombers in London. Parts of the liberal press have pondered the question of how apparently nice young people could become embroiled in such fearful events. One young man was a proficient cricketer. Another was still a teenager. The very normality of these young people is precisely what disturbs those in authority in Britain. Where else will this plague strike? Which other bright students will succumb? For their part, those who destroyed Falluja, and those who slaughtered one hundred thousand Iraqi civilians, had no need of suicide bombs. They disposed of a vast arsenal of bunker busters, and enough long-range airplanes to fly from Diego Garcia or, indeed, from England, in order to rain destruction on Iraq. As often happens, Steve Bell's cartoon says it all. Another world is certainly necessary.

But the necessity of this world is not confined to the exigencies of the war in Iraq. The most important news in today's world originates from leaks, and *The Mail on Sunday* gave us just such a leak in the document entitled "Options for future UK force posture in Iraq" (see page 61). The Secretary for Defence protested vigorously at this leak, which discusses substantial diminution of the numbers of American and British troops to be stationed in Iraq, from the beginning of 2006 onwards. Britons are becoming used to the daily leak, so that this one has received less attention than it deserves. It presumes that fourteen of Iraq's eighteen provinces could be passed over to Iraqi control within months, bringing the size of the occupation army down from 176,000 to 66,000. As ever, the subaltern role of Mr Blair's forces is confirmed in afterthoughts.

The Americans, who are the primary decision-makers on such matters, are split. The Pentagon and the Central Command favour a bold reduction in force numbers, no doubt in the secure knowledge that elections in the United States might well punish President Bush for timidity on this matter. The multinational forces in Iraq are said to be more cautious. The Bush administration is evidently optimistic, because it thinks that the conflict is confined to the Sunni territories in Iraq's heartland. The forces in theatre, however, are much less sanguine. They, after all, are the ones who are being shot at, or blown up. If anything they would like more, not fewer soldiers, to help them.

Full spectrum dominance or not, the Americans lack the troops necessary to sustain this war at the level it has already reached. National guardsmen are not re-enlisting. But the imperial appetite grows and grows. The war in Afghanistan has exploded again, and the ghost of bin Laden continues to walk on the Pakistan border. American troops are deployed in Tajikistan and Uzbekistan. Former Soviet Central Asia is turbulent, and nothing can be taken for granted there. And then, there is the impending war on Iran, for which President Bush is only too willing to talk the talk, but for which he may not quite know how to walk the walk.

In all this, Mr. Blair finds himself in an increasingly ignominious position. His all-powerful protector lacks the reach to defend him. His own population has no appetite for this war, still less for those which are planned to follow. There is a great shortage of willing soldiers.

And that is another reason why another world is necessary. If everything else were equal, the diminution of the appetite for war would be an entirely positive outcome.

But the United States has no intention of simply evacuating Iraq. Fourteen major bases are envisaged in Baghdad and at Balad, Kirkuk, Mosul, Taji, An Nasiriyah, Tikrit and Falluja, as well as between Arbil and Kirkuk. These installations will include former Iraqi military bases as well as significant air bases in Western and Northern Iraq. Occupation is scheduled to continue, but with fewer occupiers. This implies an increased reliance on mechanical soldiery, bigger and bigger bombs. And cleverer bombs, as well. Those who object will suffer condign punishment by remote control, quite possibly from space. And that is the way that war fighting is evolving. The Americans will still get their oil, their bases will still strike terror into neighbouring countries, but obedience, they think, will depend on the sophistication of the developing new hardware. New nuclear weapons, and space-based weapons, entail a bonfire of the treaties governing these things. They entail vast, and in all times of peace, pointless expenditure. But, if we voice the unspeakable, what if it were not pointless? For the British, who hold their 'deterrent' system under licence from the United States, the expenditure will prove ruinous (see page 63).

That is the context in which we have decided to reproduce in full the recent paper by Robert McNamara, 'Apocalypse Soon' (see page 7), to which we referred in Spokesman 86 (see pages 3 to 5). This is the returning age of the Bomb. The great men who seek to ride on that bomb will, of course, destroy themselves, and in that sense they, too, are suicide bombers. Dr. Strangelove, it is clear, was right. But most of us have not yet reached the point at which we are ready for suicide. There is a stubborn appetite for life, that is why there will be a new surge for peace, and for an end to nuclear weapons.

Ken Coates

BERTRAND RUSSELL

Get inside one of the greatest minds of the 20th Century

'There is no one who uses the English language more beguilingly than Russell, no one smoothes the kinks and creases more artfully out of the most crumpled weaves of thought.' – *The Times*

ABC of Relativity
Bertrand Russell
Introduction by **Peter Clark**

Bertrand Russell's most brilliant work of scientific popularisation.

Pb: 0-415-15429-4: £11.99

The Scientific Outlook
Bertrand Russell

This early classic illuminates Russell's thinking on the promise and threat of scientific progress.

Hb: 0-415-24996-1: £50.00
Pb: 0-415-24997-X: £13.99

The Collected Papers of Bertrand Russell Volume 29
NEW

Détente or Destruction, 1955-57
Bertrand Russell
Edited by **Andrew G. Bone**

Continues the publication of Routledge's multi-volume critical edition of Bertrand Russell's shorter writings.

February 2005
Hb: 0-415-35837-X: £125.00

Common Sense and Nuclear Warfare
Bertrand Russell
Introduction by
Ken Coates

This book presents Russell's keen insights into the threat of nuclear conflict, and his argument that the only way to end this threat is to end war itself.

Hb: 0415249945: £50.00
Pb: 0415249953: £9.99

Power
A New Social Analysis
Bertrand Russell
Introduction by
Samuel Brittan

In this remarkable book Russell argues that power is man's ultimate goal and is, in its many guises, the single most important element in the development of any society.

Routledge Classics series
Pb: 0-415-32507-2: £9.99

For details on our full range of Bertrand Russell titles, and how to order, please visit
www.routledge.com

For credit card orders: call +44 (0)1264 343071
or email book.orders@routledge.co.uk
For more information, or for a free Philosophy catalogue please call
Helen Lawton on 020 7017 6044 or email helen.lawton@tandf.co.uk

Routledge
Taylor & Francis Group

www.routledge.com   available from all good bookshops

Joy shall be in heaven ...

Robert S. McNamara

'What man of you, having an hundred sheep, and if he lose one of them doth not leave the ninety and nine in the wilderness, and go after that which is lost, until he find it?

And when he hath found it, he layeth it on his shoulders, rejoicing ...

... likewise joy shall be in heaven over one sinner that repenteth, more than over ninety and nine just persons which need no repentance.'

Luke, chapter 15, 4-7

In our editorial (Spokesman 86) we referred to 'Apocalypse Soon'. In view of the importance of this article, we now reproduce it in full. Robert McNamara was United States Secretary of Defence from 1961 to 1968. He was centrally involved in the Cuban Missile Crisis of 1962, and later in the war on Vietnam. From 1968 to 1981 he was President of the World Bank.

It is time – well past time, in my view – for the United States to cease its Cold War-style reliance on nuclear weapons as a foreign-policy tool. At the risk of appearing simplistic and provocative, I would characterise current US nuclear weapons policy as immoral, illegal, militarily unnecessary, and dreadfully dangerous. The risk of an accidental or inadvertent nuclear launch is unacceptably high. Far from reducing these risks, the Bush administration has signalled that it is committed to keeping the US nuclear arsenal as a mainstay of its military power – a commitment that is simultaneously eroding the international norms that have limited the spread of nuclear weapons and fissile materials for 50 years. Much of the current US nuclear policy has been in place since before I was secretary of defence, and it has only grown more dangerous and diplomatically destructive in the intervening years.

Today, the United States has deployed approximately 4,500 strategic, offensive nuclear warheads. Russia has roughly 3,800. The strategic forces of Britain, France, and China are considerably smaller, with 200-400 nuclear weapons in each state's arsenal. The new nuclear states of Pakistan and India have fewer than 100 weapons each. North Korea now claims to have developed nuclear weapons, and US intelligence agencies estimate that Pyongyang has enough fissile material for 2-8 bombs.

How destructive are these weapons? The average US warhead has a destructive power 20 times that of the Hiroshima bomb. Of the 8,000 active or operational US warheads, 2,000 are on hair-trigger alert, ready to be launched on 15 minutes' warning. How are these weapons to be used? The United States has never endorsed the policy of 'no first use,' not during my seven years as secretary or since. We have been and remain prepared to initiate the use of nuclear weapons – by the decision of one person, the president – against either a nuclear or non-nuclear enemy whenever we believe it is in our interest to do so. For decades, US nuclear forces have been sufficiently strong to absorb a first strike and then inflict 'unacceptable' damage on an opponent. This has been and (so long as we face a nuclear-armed, potential adversary) must continue to be the foundation of our nuclear deterrent.

In my time as secretary of defence, the commander of the US Strategic Air Command (SAC) carried with him a secure telephone, no matter where he went, 24 hours a day, seven days a week, 365 days a year. The telephone of the commander, whose headquarters were in Omaha, Nebraska, was linked to the underground command post of the North American Defense Command, deep inside Cheyenne Mountain, in Colorado, and to the US president, wherever he happened to be. The president always had at hand nuclear release codes in the so-called football, a briefcase carried for the president at all times by a US military officer.

The Strategic Air Command's commander's orders were to answer the telephone by no later than the end of the third ring. If it rang, and he was informed that a nuclear attack of enemy ballistic missiles appeared to be under way, he was allowed 2 to 3 minutes to decide whether the warning was valid (over the years, the United States has received many false warnings), and if so, how the United States should respond. He was then given approximately ten minutes to determine what to recommend, to locate and advise the president, permit the president to discuss the situation with two or three close advisers (presumably the secretary of defence and the chairman of the Joint Chiefs of Staff), and to receive the president's decision and pass it immediately, along with the codes, to the launch sites. The president essentially had two options: he could decide to ride out the attack and defer until later any decision to launch a retaliatory strike. Or, he could order an immediate retaliatory strike, from a menu of options, thereby launching US weapons that were targeted on the opponent's military-industrial assets. Our opponents in Moscow presumably had and have similar arrangements.

The whole situation seems so bizarre as to be beyond belief. On any given day, as we go about our business, the president is prepared to make a decision within 20 minutes that could launch one of the most devastating weapons in the world. To declare war requires an Act of Congress, but to launch a nuclear holocaust requires 20 minutes' deliberation by the president and his advisors. But that is what we have lived with for 40 years. With very few changes, this system remains largely intact, including the 'football,' the president's constant companion.

I was able to change some of these dangerous policies and procedures. My colleagues and I started arms control talks; we installed safeguards to reduce the risk of unauthorised launches; we added options to the nuclear war plans so that the president did not have to choose between an all-or-nothing response, and we eliminated the vulnerable and provocative nuclear missiles in Turkey. I wish I had done more, but we were in the midst of the Cold War, and our options were limited.

The United States and our Nato allies faced a strong Soviet and Warsaw Pact conventional threat. Many of the allies (and some in Washington as well) felt strongly that preserving the US option of launching a first strike was necessary for the sake of keeping the Soviets at bay. What is shocking is that today, more than a decade after the end of the Cold War, the basic US nuclear policy is unchanged. It has not adapted to the collapse of the Soviet Union. Plans and procedures have not been revised to make the United States or other countries less likely to push the button. At a minimum, we should remove all strategic nuclear weapons from 'hair-trigger' alert, as others have recommended, including Gen. George Lee Butler, the last commander of Strategic Air Command (see *Spokesman 63*). That simple change would greatly reduce the risk of an accidental nuclear launch. It would also signal to other states that the United States is taking steps to end its reliance on nuclear weapons.

We pledged to work in good faith toward the eventual elimination of nuclear arsenals when we negotiated the Nuclear Non-Proliferation Treaty (NPT) in 1968. In May 2005, diplomats from more than 180 nations met in New York City to review the NPT and assess whether members are living up to the agreement. The United States is focused, for understandable reasons, on persuading North Korea to rejoin the treaty and on negotiating deeper constraints on Iran's nuclear ambitions. Those states must be convinced to keep the promises they made when they originally signed the NPT – that they would not build nuclear weapons in return for access to peaceful uses of nuclear energy. But the attention of many nations, including some potential new nuclear weapons states, is also on the United States. Keeping such large numbers of weapons, and maintaining them on hair-trigger alert, are potent signs that the United States is not seriously working toward the elimination of its arsenal and raises troubling questions as to why any other state should restrain its nuclear ambitions.

A preview of the Apocalypse

The destructive power of nuclear weapons is well known, but given the United States' continued reliance on them, it's worth remembering the danger they present. A 2000 report by the International Physicians for the Prevention of Nuclear War describes the likely effects of a single one megaton weapon – dozens of which are contained in the Russian and US inventories. At ground zero, the explosion creates a crater 300 feet deep and 1,200 feet in diameter. Within one second, the atmosphere itself ignites into a fireball more than a half-mile in diameter. The surface of the fireball radiates nearly three times the light and heat of a comparable area of the surface of the sun, extinguishing in seconds all life below and radiating outward at the speed of light, causing instantaneous severe burns to people within one to three miles. A blast wave of compressed air reaches a distance of three miles in about 12 seconds, flattening factories and commercial buildings. Debris carried by winds of 250 mph inflicts lethal injuries throughout the area. At least 50 per cent of people in the area die immediately, prior to any injuries from radiation or the developing firestorm.

Of course, our knowledge of these effects is not entirely hypothetical. Nuclear weapons, with roughly one-seventieth of the power of the 1 megaton bomb just described, were twice used by the United States in August 1945. One atomic bomb was dropped on Hiroshima. Around 80,000 people died immediately; approximately 200,000 died eventually. Later, a similar size bomb was dropped on Nagasaki. On November 7, 1995, the mayor of Nagasaki recalled his memory of the attack in testimony to the International Court of Justice:

> 'Nagasaki became a city of death where not even the sound of insects could be heard. After a while, countless men, women and children began to gather for a drink of water at the banks of nearby Urakami River, their hair and clothing scorched and their burnt skin hanging off in sheets like rags. Begging for help they died one after another in the water or in heaps on the banks ... Four months after the atomic bombing, 74,000 people were dead, and 75,000 had suffered injuries, that is, two-thirds of the city population had fallen victim to this calamity that came upon Nagasaki like a preview of the Apocalypse.'

Why did so many civilians have to die? Because the civilians, who made up nearly 100 percent of the victims of Hiroshima and Nagasaki, were unfortunately 'co-located' with Japanese military and industrial targets. Their annihilation, though not the objective of those dropping the bombs, was an inevitable result of the choice of those targets. It is worth noting that during the Cold War, the United States reportedly had dozens of nuclear warheads targeted on Moscow alone, because it contained so many military targets and so much 'industrial capacity.'

Presumably, the Soviets similarly targeted many US cities. The statement that our nuclear weapons do not target populations *per se* was and remains totally misleading in the sense that the so-called collateral damage of large nuclear strikes would include tens of millions of innocent civilian dead. This in a nutshell is what nuclear weapons do: they indiscriminately blast, burn, and irradiate with a speed and finality that are almost incomprehensible. This is exactly what countries like the United States and Russia, with nuclear weapons on hair-trigger alert, continue to threaten every minute of every day in this new 21st century.

No way to win

I have worked on issues relating to United States and Nato nuclear strategy and war plans for more than 40 years. During that time, I have never seen a piece of paper that outlined a plan for the United States or Nato to initiate the use of nuclear weapons with any benefit for the United States or Nato. I have made this statement in front of audiences, including Nato defence ministers and senior military leaders, many times. No one has ever refuted it. To launch weapons against a nuclear-equipped opponent would be suicidal. To do so against a non-nuclear enemy would be militarily unnecessary, morally repugnant, and politically indefensible.

I reached these conclusions very soon after becoming secretary of defence. Although I believe Presidents John F. Kennedy and Lyndon Johnson shared my view, it was impossible for any of us to make such statements publicly because they were totally contrary to established Nato policy. After leaving the Defence Department, I became president of the World Bank. During my 13-year tenure, from 1968 to 1981, I was prohibited, as an employee of an international institution, from commenting publicly on issues of US national security. After my retirement from the bank, I began to reflect on how I, with seven years' experience as secretary of defence, might contribute to an understanding of the issues with which I began my public service career.

At that time, much was being said and written regarding how the United States could, and why it should, be able to fight and win a nuclear war with the Soviets. This view implied, of course, that nuclear weapons did have military utility; that they could be used in battle with ultimate gain to whoever had the largest force or used them with the greatest acumen. Having studied these views, I decided to go public with some information that I knew would be controversial, but that I felt was needed to inject reality into these increasingly unreal discussions about the military utility of nuclear weapons. In articles and speeches, I criticised the fundamentally flawed assumption that nuclear weapons could be used in some limited way. There is no way to effectively contain a nuclear strike – to keep it from inflicting enormous destruction on civilian life and property, and there is no guarantee against unlimited escalation once the first nuclear strike occurs. We cannot avoid the serious and unacceptable risk of nuclear war until we recognise these facts and base our military plans and policies upon this recognition. I hold these views even more strongly today than I did when I first spoke out against the nuclear dangers our policies were creating. I know from direct experience that US nuclear policy today creates unacceptable risks to other nations and to our own.

What Castro taught us

Among the costs of maintaining nuclear weapons is the risk – to me an unacceptable risk – of use of the weapons either by accident or as a result of misjudgment or miscalculation in times of crisis. The Cuban Missile Crisis demonstrated that the United States and the Soviet Union – and indeed the rest of the world – came within a hair's breadth of nuclear disaster in October 1962.

Indeed, according to former Soviet military leaders, at the height of the crisis, Soviet forces in Cuba possessed 162 nuclear warheads, including at least 90 tactical warheads. At about the same time, Cuban President Fidel Castro asked the Soviet ambassador to Cuba to send a cable to Soviet Premier Nikita Khrushchev stating that Castro urged him to counter a US attack with a nuclear response. Clearly, there was a high risk that in the face of a US attack, which many in the US government were prepared to recommend to President Kennedy, the Soviet forces in Cuba would have decided to use their nuclear weapons rather than lose them. Only a few years ago did we learn that the four Soviet submarines trailing the US Naval vessels near Cuba each carried torpedoes with nuclear warheads. Each of the sub commanders had the authority to launch his torpedoes. The situation was even more frightening because, as the lead commander recounted to me, the subs were out of communication with their Soviet bases, and they continued their patrols for four days after Khrushchev announced the withdrawal of the missiles from Cuba.

The lesson, if it had not been clear before, was made so at a conference on the crisis held in Havana in 1992, when we first began to learn from former Soviet officials about their preparations for nuclear war in the event of a US invasion. Near the end of that meeting, I asked Castro whether he would have recommended that Khrushchev use the weapons in the face of a US invasion, and if so, how he thought the United States would respond. 'We started from the assumption that if there was an invasion of Cuba, nuclear war would erupt,' Castro replied. 'We were certain of that.... [W]e would be forced to pay the price that we would disappear.' He continued, 'Would I have been ready to use nuclear weapons? Yes, I would have agreed to the use of nuclear weapons.' And he added, 'If Mr. McNamara or Mr. Kennedy had been in our place, and had their country been invaded, or their country was going to be occupied ... I believe they would have used tactical nuclear weapons.'

I hope that President Kennedy and I would not have behaved as Castro suggested we would have. His decision would have destroyed his country. Had we responded in a similar way the damage to the United States would have been unthinkable. But human beings are fallible. In conventional war, mistakes cost lives, sometimes thousands of lives. However, if mistakes were to affect decisions relating to the use of nuclear forces, there would be no learning curve. They would result in the destruction of nations. The indefinite combination of human fallibility and nuclear weapons carries a very high risk of nuclear catastrophe. There is no way to reduce the risk to acceptable levels, other than to first eliminate the hair-trigger alert policy and later to eliminate or nearly eliminate nuclear weapons. The United States should move immediately to institute these actions, in cooperation with Russia. That is the lesson of the Cuban Missile Crisis.

A dangerous obsession

On November 13, 2001, President George W. Bush announced that he had told Russian President Vladimir Putin that the United States would reduce 'operationally deployed nuclear warheads' from approximately 5,300 to a level between 1,700 and 2,200 over the next decade. This scaling back would approach the 1,500 to 2,200 range that Putin had proposed for Russia. However, the Bush administration's Nuclear Posture Review, mandated by the US Congress and issued in January 2002, presents quite a different story. It assumes that strategic offensive nuclear weapons in much larger numbers than 1,700 to 2,200 will be part of US military forces for the next several decades. Although the number of deployed warheads will be reduced to 3,800 in 2007 and to between 1,700 and 2,200 by 2012, the warheads and many of the launch vehicles taken off deployment will be maintained in a 'responsive' reserve from which they could be moved back to the operationally deployed force. The Nuclear Posture Review received little attention from the media. But its emphasis on strategic offensive nuclear weapons deserves vigorous public scrutiny. Although any proposed reduction is welcome, it is doubtful that survivors – if there were any – of an exchange of 3,200 warheads (the US and Russian numbers projected for 2012), with a destructive power approximately 65,000 times that of the Hiroshima bomb, could detect a difference between the effects of such an exchange and one that would result from the launch of the current US and Russian forces totalling about 12,000 warheads.

In addition to projecting the deployment of large numbers of strategic nuclear weapons far into the future, the Bush administration is planning an extensive and expensive series of programmes to sustain and modernise the existing nuclear force and to begin studies for new launch vehicles, as well as new warheads for all of the launch platforms. Some members of the administration have called for new nuclear weapons that could be used as bunker busters against underground shelters (such as the shelters Saddam Hussein used in Baghdad). New production facilities for fissile materials would need to be built to support the expanded force. The plans provide for integrating a national ballistic missile defence into the new triad of offensive weapons to enhance the nation's ability to use its 'power projection forces' by improving our ability to counterattack an enemy. The Bush administration also announced that it has no intention to ask Congress to ratify the Comprehensive Test Ban Treaty (CTBT), and, though no decision to test has been made, the administration has ordered the national laboratories to begin research on new nuclear weapons designs and to prepare the underground test sites in Nevada for nuclear tests if necessary in the future. Clearly, the Bush administration assumes that nuclear weapons will be part of US military forces for at least the next several decades.

Good faith participation in international negotiation on nuclear disarmament – including participation in the Comprehensive Test Ban Treaty – is a legal and political obligation of all parties to the Non-Proliferation Treaty that entered into force in 1970 and was extended indefinitely in 1995. The Bush administration's nuclear programme, alongside its refusal to ratify the Comprehensive Test Ban Treaty, will be viewed, with reason, by many nations as equivalent to a US break from the treaty. It says to the non-nuclear weapons nations, 'We, with the strongest conventional military force in the world, require nuclear weapons in perpetuity, but you, facing potentially well-armed opponents, are never to be allowed even one nuclear weapon.'

If the United States continues its current nuclear stance, over time, substantial proliferation of nuclear weapons will almost surely follow. Some, or all, of such nations as Egypt, Japan, Saudi Arabia, Syria, and Taiwan will very likely initiate nuclear weapons programmes, increasing both the risk of use of the weapons and the diversion of weapons and fissile materials into the hands of rogue states or terrorists. Diplomats and intelligence agencies believe Osama bin Laden has made several attempts to acquire nuclear weapons or fissile materials. It has been widely reported that Sultan Bashiruddin Mahmood, former director of Pakistan's nuclear reactor complex, met with bin Laden several times. Were al Qaeda to acquire fissile materials, especially enriched uranium, its ability to produce nuclear weapons would be great. The knowledge of how to construct a simple gun-type nuclear device, like the one we dropped on Hiroshima, is now widespread. Experts have little doubt that terrorists could construct such a primitive device if they acquired the requisite enriched uranium material. Indeed, just last summer, at a meeting of the National Academy of Sciences, former Secretary of Defence William J. Perry said, 'I have never been more fearful of a nuclear detonation than now ... There is a greater than 50 percent probability of a nuclear strike on US targets within a decade.' I share his fears.

We are at a critical moment in human history – perhaps not as dramatic as that of the Cuban Missile Crisis, but a moment no less crucial. Neither the Bush administration, the Congress, the American people, nor the people of other nations have debated the merits of alternative, long-range nuclear weapons policies for their countries or the world. They have not examined the military utility of the weapons; the risk of inadvertent or accidental use; the moral and legal considerations relating to the use or threat of use of the weapons; or the impact of current policies on proliferation. Such debates are long overdue. If they are held, I believe they will conclude, as have I and an increasing number of senior military leaders, politicians, and civilian security experts: we must move promptly towards the elimination – or near elimination – of all nuclear weapons. For many, there is a strong temptation to cling to the strategies of the past 40 years. But to do so would be a serious mistake leading to unacceptable risks for all nations.

Reproduced with permission from FOREIGN POLICY 149 (July/August 2005) www.foreignpolicy.com. Copyright 2005, Carnegie Endowment for International Peace.

TRANSPORT & GENERAL WORKERS' UNION
London, South East & East Anglia

In this anniversary year - no more nukes no son of Star Wars

Eddie McDermott
Regional Secretary

John Childs
Regional Chair

(phone)
020 8800 4281

(e-mail)
emcdermott@tgwu.org.uk

(fax)
020 8802 8388

The Final Abyss?

*Admiral of the Fleet
The Earl Mountbatten
of Burma*

Lord Mountbatten's landmark statement that the 'nuclear arms race has no military purpose' was made in Strasbourg in 1979, in the context of Cold War plans to deploy new 'theatre' nuclear weapons in Europe. We first published it the following year in a little book called Apocalypse Now? *(Spokesman Books £4.95). We re-publish it 25 years later, at a time when Robert McNamara has warned of the danger of 'Apocalypse Soon', as the nuclear arms race accelerates again, and the United States prepares to resume nuclear testing.*

Do the frightening facts about the arms race, which show that we are rushing headlong towards a precipice, make any of those responsible for this disastrous course pull themselves together and reach for the brakes?

The answer is 'no' and I only wish that I could be the bearer of the glad tidings that there has been a change of attitude and we are beginning to see a steady rate of disarmament. Alas, that is not the case.

I am deeply saddened when I reflect on how little has been achieved in spite of all the talk there has been particularly about nuclear disarmament. There have been numerous international conferences and negotiations on the subject and we have all nursed dreams of a world at peace but to no avail. Since the end of the Second World War, 34 years ago, we have had war after war. There is still armed conflict going on in several parts of the world. We live in an age of extreme peril because every war today carries the danger that it could spread and involve the super powers.

And here lies the greatest danger of all. A military confrontation between the nuclear powers could entail the horrifying risk of nuclear warfare. The Western powers and the USSR started by producing and stockpiling nuclear weapons as a deterrent to general war. The idea seemed simple enough. Because of the enormous amount of destruction that could be wreaked by a single nuclear explosion, the idea was that both sides in what we still see as an East-West conflict would be deterred from taking any aggressive action which might endanger the vital interests of the other.

It was not long, however, before smaller nuclear weapons of various designs were produced and deployed for use in what was assumed to be a tactical or theatre war. The belief was that were hostilities ever to break out in Western Europe, such weapons could be used in field warfare without triggering an all-out nuclear exchange leading to the final holocaust.

I have never found this idea credible. I have never been able to accept the reasons for the belief that any class of nuclear weapons can be categorised in terms of their tactical or strategic purposes.

Next month I enter my eightieth year. I am one of the few survivors of the First World War who rose to high command in the Second and I know how impossible it is to pursue military operations in accordance with fixed plans and agreements. In warfare the unexpected is the rule and no one can anticipate what an opponent's reaction will be to the unexpected.

As a sailor I saw enough death and destruction at sea but I also had the opportunity of seeing the absolute destruction of the war zone of the western front in the First World War, where those who fought in the trenches had an average expectation of life of only a few weeks.

Then in 1943 I became Supreme Allied Commander in South East Asia and saw death and destruction on an even greater scale. But that was all conventional warfare and, horrible as it was, we all felt we had a 'fighting' chance of survival. In the event of a nuclear war there will be no chances, there will be no survivors – all will be obliterated.

I am not asserting this without having deeply thought about the matter. When I was Chief of the British Defence Staff I made my views known. I have heard the arguments against this view but I have never found them convincing. So I repeat in all sincerity as a military man I can see no use for any nuclear weapons which would not end in escalation, with consequences that no one can conceive.

And nuclear devastation is not science fiction – it is a matter of fact. Thirty-four years ago there was the terrifying experience of the two atomic bombs that effaced the cities of Hiroshima and Nagasaki off the map. In describing the nightmare a Japanese journalist wrote as follows:

> 'Suddenly a glaring whitish, pinkish light appeared in the sky accompanied by an unnatural tremor which was followed almost immediately by a wave of suffocating heat and a wind which swept away everything in its path. Within a few seconds the thousands of people in the streets in the centre of the town were scorched by a wave of searing heat. Many were killed instantly, others lay writhing on the ground screaming in agony from the intolerable pain of their burns. Everything standing upright in the way of the blast – walls, houses, factories and other buildings, was annihilated ... Hiroshima had ceased to exist'.

But that is not the end of the story. We remember the tens of thousands who were killed instantly or worse still those who suffered a slow painful death from the effect of the burns – we forget that many are still dying horribly from the delayed effects of radiation. To this knowledge must be added the fact that we now have missiles a thousand times as dreadful; I repeat, a thousand times as horrible.

One or two nuclear strikes on this great city of Strasbourg with what today would be regarded as relatively low yield weapons would utterly destroy all that we see around us and immediately kill probably half of its population. Imagine what the picture would be if larger nuclear strikes were to be levelled against not just Strasbourg but ten other cities in, say, a 200 mile radius. Or even worse, imagine what the picture would be if there was an unrestrained exchange of nuclear weapons – and this is the most appalling risk of all since, as I have already said, I cannot imagine a situation in which nuclear weapons would be used as battlefield weapons without the conflagration spreading.

Could we not take steps to make sure that these things never come about? A new world war can hardly fail to involve the all-out use of nuclear weapons. Such a war would not drag on for years. It could all be over in a matter of days.

And when it is all over what will the world be like? Our fine great buildings, our homes will exist no more. The thousands of years it took to develop our civilisation will have been in vain. Our works of art will be lost. Radio, television, newspapers will disappear. There will be no means of transport. There will be no hospitals. No help can be expected for the few mutilated survivors in any town to be sent from a neighbouring town – there will be no neighbouring towns left, no neighbours, there will be no help, there will be no hope.

How can we stand by and do nothing to prevent the destruction of our world? Einstein, whose centenary we celebrate this year, was asked to prophesy what weapons would be used in the Third World War. I am told he replied to the following effect:

> 'On the assumption that a Third World War must escalate to nuclear destruction, I can tell you what the Fourth World War will be fought with – bows and arrows'!

The facts about the global nuclear arms race are well known and as I have already said the Stockholm International Peace Research Institute has played its part in disseminating authoritative material on world armaments and the need for international efforts to reduce them. But how do we set about achieving practical measures of nuclear arms control and disarmament?

To begin with we are most likely to preserve the peace if there is a military balance of strength between East and West. The real need is for both sides to replace the attempts to maintain a balance through ever-increasing and even more costly nuclear armaments by a balance based on mutual restraint. Better still, by reduction of nuclear armaments I believe it should be possible to achieve greater security at a lower level of military confrontation.

I regret enormously the delays which the Americans and Russians have experienced in reaching a SALT II agreement [Strategic Arms Limitation Talks II] for the limitation of even one major class of nuclear weapons with which it deals. I regret even more the fact that opposition to reaching any agreement which will bring about a restraint in the production and deployment of nuclear weapons is becoming so powerful in the United States. What can their motives be?

As a militaryman who has given half a century of active Service I say in all sincerity that the nuclear arms race has no military purpose. Wars cannot be fought with nuclear weapons. Their existence only adds to our perils because of the illusions which they have generated.

There are powerful voices around the world who still give credence to the old Roman precept – if you desire peace, prepare for war. This is absolute nuclear nonsense and I repeat – it is a disastrous misconception to believe that by increasing the total uncertainty one increases one's own certainty.

This year we have already seen the beginnings of a miracle. Through the courageous determination of Presidents Carter and Sadat and Prime Minister Begin we have seen the first real move towards what we all hope will be a lasting peace between Egypt and Israel. Their journey has only just begun and the path they have chosen will be long and fraught with disappointments and obstacles. But these bold leaders have realised the alternative and have faced up to their duty in a way which those of us who hunger for the peace of the world applaud.

Is it possible that this initiative will lead to the start of yet another even more vital miracle and someone somewhere will take that first step along the long stony road which will lead us to an effective form of nuclear arms limitation, including the banning of Tactical Nuclear Weapons?

After all it is true that science offers us almost unlimited opportunities but it is up to us, the people, to make the moral and philosophical choices and since the threat to humanity is the work of human beings, it is up to man to save himself from himself.

The world now stands on the brink of the final Abyss. Let us all resolve to take all possible practical steps to ensure that we do not, through our own folly, go over the edge.

www.impeachBlair.org

A Case to Answer

£5.00

A Case to Answer

A first report on the potential impeachment of the Prime Minister for High Crimes and Misdemeanours in relation to the invasion of Iraq

by Glen Rangwala & Dan Plesch for Adam Price MP

With Legal Opinion by Rabinder Singh QC & Professor Conor Gearty

Spokesman Books, Russell House,
Bulwell Lane, Nottingham,
NG6 0BT, England
Tel: 0115 9708318 - Fax: 0115 9420433
email: elfeuro@compuserve.com
www.spokesmanbooks.com
Credit/Debit cards accepted

SPOKESMAN imprint of the
Bertrand Russell Peace Foundation

The Nuclear Future?

Zia Mian

Zia Mian left England for the United States some years ago, and now teaches at Princeton University.

Many events commemorating the 60th anniversary of the defeat of Nazi Germany in the Second World War were held this past May. Yet there has been little or no discussion of some of the most important and enduring legacies of that war, legacies that have cast long shadows ever since. Nationalism, industrial production, the bureau-cratic state, and science and technology were harnessed to the cause of war in terrible new ways. It brought us the gas chambers, the systematic bombing of cities, and nuclear weapons. These three forms of modern violence are different in some significant ways, but they shared important features. Among these were centralised authority, extensive compartmentalisation of responsibilities, tasks, and knowledge accompanied by strong organisational loyalty, along with scientific rationalisation for the policy, and technical ways of distancing perpetrators from victims.

Many moral barriers were breached, and not all were by the Nazis. In September 1939, US President Franklin Roosevelt denounced the bombing of cities and appealed to the leaders of Germany, Britain, France, Italy, and Poland to desist. Roosevelt wrote to them that 'The ruthless bombing from the air of civilians in unfortified centres of population during the course of the hostilities' had 'sickened the hearts of every civilised man and woman, and has profoundly shocked the conscience of humanity.' He said:

> 'If resort is had to this form of inhuman barbarism during the period of the tragic conflagration with which the world is now confronted, hundreds of thousands of innocent human beings who have no responsibility for, and who are not even remotely participating in, the hostilities which have now broken out, will lose their lives. I am therefore addressing this urgent appeal to every government which may be engaged in hostilities publicly to affirm its determination that its armed forces shall in no event, and under no circumstances, undertake the bombardment from the air of civilian populations or of unfortified cities.'

While no American city was ever subject to such bombardment, when America entered the war it joined Britain in the bombing of German cities. Then it bombed Japanese cities. In a recent film, *The Fog of War*, former US Secretary of Defence Robert McNamara explains that the US bombing campaign killed 50 to 90 per cent of the people in 67 Japanese cities. This does not include the use of the atom bomb on Hiroshima and Nagasaki.

The most profound moral threshold that was crossed in the Second World War was in the effort to build the first atomic bomb. Its use in the war, and the nuclear age that followed, showed just how far things had gone. Seven years after India and Pakistan tested their nuclear weapons (on May 11 and 13, and May 28 and 30, 1998), it is worth asking what barriers have been and are being crossed in the subcontinent.

Early experiments

There is no doubt that the scientists who built the first atom bomb knew they were preparing a weapon of mass destruction. One particular incident sheds light on the scale of destruction these scientists may have been contemplating. In April 1943, the Italian physicist Enrico Fermi proposed to Robert Oppenheimer, the scientific head of the US atomic bomb programme, that a nuclear reactor might be used to produce radioactive isotopes not just for the bomb, but in large quantities to poison German food supplies. Oppenheimer found the idea 'promising.' But, Oppenheimer wrote to Fermi, 'We should not attempt a plan unless we can poison food sufficient to kill half a million men.'

Other kinds of violence were unleashed, too. As part of the Manhattan Project, scientists were working with unprecedented amounts and kinds of radioactive materials. They needed to know what levels of radiation exposure might be safe and what would be fatal for scientists and engineers on the project, if no one else. They started to create knowledge about radiation effects on health. They started by irradiating animals. But this was only the beginning. In the next thirty years, over 23,000 people in the United States were the subjects for 1,400 radiation experiments, in many cases without their informed consent. When details were released in December 1993, US Secretary of Energy Hazel O'Leary was moved to exclaim that, 'The only thing I could think of was Nazi Germany.'

On 16 July 1945, the world's first atomic explosion burst over the New Mexico desert. The Trinity test was conducted at a place fatefully called Jornada del Muerto (the Journey of Death). Robert Oppenheimer watched the test and famously declared 'I am become death, the destroyer of worlds.' The physicist I. I. Rabi had a similar but less known reflection about what scientists, including himself, had wrought:

> 'At first I was thrilled. It was a vision. Then a few minutes afterwards, I had gooseflesh all over me when I realised what this meant for the future of humanity. Up until then, humanity was, after all, a limited factor in the evolution and process of nature. The vast oceans, lakes and rivers, the atmosphere were not very much affected by the existence of mankind. The new powers represented a threat not only to mankind but to all forms of life: the seas and the air. One could foresee that nothing was immune from the tremendous power of these new forces.'

The United States used its atomic bombs to destroy the Japanese city of Hiroshima, on 6 August 1945, and the city of Nagasaki on 9 August. Over 200,000 people died immediately or within weeks from injuries. More died in subsequent months and years; the exact toll is not known. In announcing the first use of the atom bomb, President Harry Truman warned on 6 August:

> 'We are now prepared to obliterate more rapidly and completely every productive enterprise the Japanese have above ground in any city... If they do not now accept our terms they may expect a rain of ruin from the air, the like of which has never been seen on this earth.'

Violence begets violence and fear. In August 1949 the Soviet Union detonated its first atomic bomb. There was a secret debate within the US government about what should be the appropriate response to the Soviet atomic bomb test, in particular whether the United States should pursue the development of an even more powerful bomb, a hydrogen bomb based on thermonuclear fusion (India claimed to test just such a bomb on 11 May 1998).

The committee that was set up to consider the possibility of a hydrogen bomb included Robert Oppenheimer, Enrico Fermi, and I. I. Rabi, among others. They concluded that the H-bomb could probably be built within five years, but advised against it. The committee argued that 'it is clear that the use of this weapon would bring about the destruction of innumerable human lives ... Its use therefore carries much further than the atomic bomb itself the policy of exterminating civilian populations.'

Debating the H-Bomb

While it was clear that the atom bomb was a tool for a policy of extermination, the committee was divided however on how to characterise the exterminist nature of an H-bomb. The majority of the committee members argued that, 'its use would involve a decision to slaughter a vast number of civilians...Therefore, a super bomb might become a weapon of genocide.' The minority view on the committee was that this statement did not go far enough. They argued,

> 'It is clear that the use of such a weapon cannot be justified on any ethical ground which gives a human being a certain individuality and dignity even if he happens to be a resident of an enemy country. The fact that no limits exist to the destructiveness of this weapon makes its very existence and the knowledge of its construction a danger to humanity as a whole. It is necessarily an evil thing considered in any light.'

The advice of the committee was rejected. The political, military, and institutional pressures of the growing nuclear complex and the Cold War prevailed. On 1 November 1952, the United States tested the first H-bomb. The Mike test, at Enewetak Atoll in the Pacific, had an explosive yield of over ten megatons. This was many hundreds of times more powerful than the bombs that destroyed Hiroshima and Nagasaki, and more explosive power than all the bombs dropped by US and British armed forces during the Second World War.

Where the United States led, others followed. The nuclear stockpiles that were manufactured by the United States and Soviet Union, and the smaller nuclear weapon states, quickly surpassed the dangers posed by earlier measures of genocide. By 1960, only 15 years after the end of the Second World War, the United States had a nuclear war plan that would have resulted in the deaths of an estimated 360-525 million people. Robert McNamara, then defence secretary, argued in 1962 that a 'reasonable' goal for nuclear war against the Soviet Union could be the destruction of 25 per cent of its population (i.e. the deaths of 55 million people) and more than two-thirds of its industrial capacity.

Recent calculations have shown that McNamara's criteria of killing 25 per cent of the Russian population would now require only 51 modern US nuclear warheads. Estimates of current arsenals in 2005 suggest that the United States has about 5,300 operational nuclear warheads (and another 5,000 on reserve), while Russia has 7,200 warheads, China has about 400, France has 350, and Britain has 200 warheads. Israel is believed to have up to 200 nuclear weapons. It is estimated India and Pakistan so far have less than 100 warheads each.

There is little solace to be had in the relatively smaller arsenals of India and Pakistan. A nuclear war between Pakistan and India in which each used only five of their nuclear weapons (each of which typically has the same yield of the bombs that destroyed Hiroshima and Nagasaki) would likely kill about three million people and severely injure another one and a half million.

The nuclear future

It is clear now that for the United States and a handful of other like-minded states, nuclear weapons have a role to play in the 21st century. While some states pursue a nuclear weapons capability, US nuclear weapons designers and military planners are pushing for new weapons designs and missions. There are arguments for new bunker-buster nuclear weapons, for more reliable nuclear weapons (that will last longer), and for nuclear weapons that will be customised in their effects.

Stephen Younger, director of the Defence Threat Reduction Agency and former associate laboratory director for nuclear weapons at Los Alamos National Laboratory, has argued that in the post-Cold War world, the United States needs new kinds of low-yield nuclear weapons because it faces 'new threats,' and the continued US 'reliance on high-yield strategic (nuclear) weapons could lead to self-deterrence, a limitation of strategic options.' Paul Robinson, the former director of Sandia National Laboratory and chairman of the policy subcommittee of the strategic advisory group for the commanders-in-chief of the US Strategic Command, has proposed developing a special low-yield 'To Whom It May Concern' nuclear arsenal, directed at third world countries. This is by no means the first time such suggestions have come from US weapons laboratories. In 1970, Harold Agnew, director of Los Alamos National Laboratory, suggested that 'if people would prepare the right spectrum of tactical weapons, we might be able to knock off this sort of foolishness we now have in Vietnam and West Asia or any place else'.

The United States is renewing its embrace of a nuclear arsenal in the post-Cold

War world, knowing that this more deeply embeds nuclear weapons in national and international structures of political and military thinking and action. The deep-seated reasons for this folly may lie in the bomb itself. The American novelist E. L. Doctorow observed that 'We have had the bomb on our minds since 1945. It was first our weaponry and then our diplomacy, and now it's our economy. How can we suppose that something so monstrously powerful would not, after years, compose our identity?'

DowningStreetGate

The Dodgiest Dossier

Brings together for the first time all the leaked memoranda about the British Government's decision to go to war on Iraq, plus the Attorney General's legal advice. There is now a lively possibility of the impeachment of President Bush, arising from the publication of the briefing papers which were leaked in the *Sunday Times* immediately before the British General Election. These papers show in graphic detail how weak was the pre-war evidence for attacking Iraq.

Price £4.00 plus £1.00 postage and packing | ISBN 0 85124 712 1
Available from **Spokesman Books, Russell House, Bulwell Lane,
Nottingham NG6 0BT, England.**
Tel: 0115 970 8318 - Fax: 0115 9420433 - email: elfeuro@compuserve.com
www.spokesmanbooks.com
credit/debit cards welcome

Kurt Vonnegut – Three Poems

SONG OF THE FLAMING NEUTER

I am as celibate as fifty per cent
of the heterosexual Roman Catholic clergy.
When my 'tantrum', what I call my TV,
flashes boobs and smiles in my face, and tells me
everybody but me is going to get laid tonight,
and this is a national emergency,
so I've got to rush out and buy a car or pills,
or a folding gymnasium I can hide under my bed,
I laugh like a hyena.

You know and I know that millions of good Americans,
present company not excepted,
are not going to get laid tonight. And we neuters vote!
I look forward to the day when our President,
who probably isn't going to get laid that night, either,
declares a National Neuter Pride Day.
And out of our closets we will come in droves, unashamed,
chins high, shoulders squared, to march up Main Streets
all over this boob-crazed land of ours, laughing like hyenas.

Limp dicks as far as the eye can see!
Long may they wave.

INTELLIGENT DESIGN

Evolution knows exactly
what it is doing,
and why.
That's how come
we've got giraffes
and the clap.

NEOCONS

I feel as though we have been invaded
by body-snatchers or Martians.
Sometimes I wish we had been.
Isn't it time somebody investigated
Yale University?

Albert Einstein

Bertrand Russell

In Spokesman 85 we marked the fiftieth anniversary of the Russell-Einstein Manifesto for nuclear disarmament, which falls in 2005. It is also fifty years since Einstein's death. Immediately before he died, he signed the Manifesto, as Russell explains in this brief memoir, written at the request of Otto Nathan, the editor of a major collection of Einstein's writings on peace, which was published posthumously in 1960.

It is a very good thing that Einstein's letters and writings on other than scientific subjects are being collected and printed. Einstein was not only the ablest man of science of his generation, he was also a wise man, which is something different. If statesmen had listened to him, the course of human events would have been less disastrous than it has been. It is the custom among those who are called 'practical' men to condemn any man capable of a wide survey as a visionary: no man is thought worthy of a voice in politics unless he ignores or does not know nine tenths of the most important relevant facts. On this ground, no one listened to Einstein. In Germany, during Hitler's reign, the theory of relativity was condemned as a Jewish trick of which the sole purpose was to bewilder Aryans. It seems that Hitler and Himmler could not understand it and rashly inferred that *no* Aryan could. In the United States, where he lived after Germany had rejected him, he received, as a scientist, all that great measure of honour which was his due; but, when he allowed himself to say anything about political matters, what he said was, by most people, considered highly undesirable.

I was among those who almost always agreed with him. He and I both opposed the First World War but considered the Second unavoidable. He and I were equally perturbed by the awful prospect of H-bomb warfare. We agreed to make a joint pronouncement on this subject in conjunction with many eminent men of science who were willing to co-operate. I drew up a statement and sent it to Einstein. Before getting an answer from him, while travelling by air from Rome to Paris, I learned of his death. On arrival in Paris, I found his letter agreeing to sign. This must have been one of the last acts of his life.

We met from time to time, but I did not see much of him except while I was living in Princeton in 1943. At that time I used to go to his house once a week to discuss various matters in the philosophy of science with him and Pauli and Gödel. Pauli and Gödel are both very eminent in their respective fields, but Einstein was, of course, outstanding even amongst the most eminent. I found these informal discussions very illuminating and exceedingly valuable.

Einstein's attitude as regards the acceptance or rejection of a scientific theory was very different from that recommended by Francis Bacon. One must, of course, know the facts. But a theory, if it is to have any value, must not emerge from careful collection and collation of individual observations. It must emerge, rather, as a sudden imaginative insight, like that of a poet or composer. When Eddington undertook to verify Einstein's predictions by observations of the eclipse of 1919, Einstein was much less interested in the result than Eddington was. I was reminded of the story about a female admirer of Whistler who told him that she had seen Battersea Bridge looking just as it did in one of his pictures, to which Whistler replied, 'Ah, Nature's coming on!' One felt that Einstein thought the solar system was 'coming on' when it decided to confirm his predictions. It is difficult to turn Einstein's method into a set of textbook maxims for the guidance of students. The recipe would have read as follows: 'First acquire a transcendent genius and an all-embracing imagination, then learn your subject, and then wait for illumination.' It is the first part of this recipe that offers difficulties.

Einstein was an extraordinarily satisfactory human being. In spite of his genius and fame, he always behaved with complete simplicity and never seemed to be claiming any superiority. His work and his violin brought him, I believe, a considerable measure of happiness, but his wide sympathies and his concern with the destiny of mankind prevented him from acquiring an undue measure of serenity. I never saw in him any trace, however faint, of vanity or envy, which are vices to which even the greatest men, such as Newton and Leibniz, are prone.

Einstein, throughout his life, cared for the individual and for individual liberty. He showed, himself, all the courage that his circumstances demanded and called upon others, often without success, to show equal courage. He had seen individual freedom lost in Germany with the advent of the Nazis, and he was quickly perceptive of any danger of a like disaster in other countries. He had small respect for the Big Battalions, and his attitude to governments was very like that of the Hebrew prophets. He was not only a great scientist but a great man, a man whom it is good to have known and consoling to contemplate.

Rudyard Kipling – A Message to New Labour

For Reg Keys

THEY shall not return to us, the resolute, the young
    The eager and whole-hearted whom we gave:
But the men who left them thriftily to die in their own dung,
    Shall they come with years and honour to the grave?

They shall not return to us, the strong men coldly slain
    In sight of help denied from day to day:
But the men who edged their agonies and chid them in their pain,
    Are they too strong and wise to put away?

Our dead shall not return to us while Day and Night divide–
    Never while the bars of sunset hold.
But the idle-minded overlings who quibbled while they died,
    Shall they thrust for high employments as of old?

Shall we only threaten and be angry for an hour?
    When the storm is ended shall we find
How softly but how swiftly they have sidled back to power
    By the favour and contrivance of their kind?

Even while they soothe us, while they promise large amends,
    Even while they make a show of fear,
Do they call upon their debtors, and take council with their friends,
    To confirm and re-establish each career?

Their lives cannot repay us—their death could not undo–
    The shame that they have laid upon our race.
But the slothfulness that wasted and the arrogance that slew,
    Shall we leave it unabated in its place?

Mesopotamia 1917

The World Tribunal on Iraq

The World Tribunal on Iraq met in the grounds of the Topkapi Palace in Istanbul from 23 to 27 June 2005. This, the culminating session of sixteen hearings around the world, brought together hundreds of participants from many countries. They included Iraqis who gave first-hand testimony of what is happening to their country under occupation. They were joined by many more advocates who addressed the causes and consequences of the war on Iraq, and answered the questions of the Tribunal's Jury of Conscience. The Jury's preliminary declaration is available online, together with many of the papers that were presented in Istanbul (see www.worldtribunal.org).

How many more tragedies?

The records have to be kept and, by definition, the perpetrators, far from keeping records, try to destroy them. They are killers of the innocent and of memory. The records are required to inspire still further the mounting opposition to the new global tyranny. The new tyrants, incomparably over-armed, can win every war – both military and economic. Yet they are losing the war (this is how they call it) of communication. They are not winning the support of world public opinion. More and more people are saying NO. Finally this will be the tyranny's undoing. But after how many more tragedies, invasions and collateral disasters? After how much more of the new poverty the tyranny engenders? Hence the urgency of keeping records, of remembering, of assembling the evidence, so that the accusations become unforgettable, and proverbial on every continent. More and more people are going to say NO, for this is the precondition today for saying YES to all we are determined to save and everything we love.

John Berger
18.06.2003
Paris-Mieussy

The Age of Irony

Arundhati Roy

This is the culminating session of the World Tribunal on Iraq. It is of particular significance that it is being held here in Turkey where the United States used Turkish air bases to launch numerous bombing missions to degrade Iraq's defences before the March 2003 invasion and has sought and continues to seek political support from the Turkish government, which it regards as an ally. All this was done in the face of enormous popular opposition by the Turkish people. As a spokesperson for the Jury of Conscience, it would make me uneasy if I did not mention that the government of India is also, like the government of Turkey, positioning itself as an 'ally' of the United States in its economic policies and the so-called War on Terror.

The testimonies at the previous sessions of the World Tribunal on Iraq in Brussels and New York have demonstrated that even those of us who have tried to follow the war in Iraq closely are not aware of a fraction of the horrors that have been unleashed in Iraq.

The Jury of Conscience at this tribunal is not here to deliver a simple verdict of guilty or not guilty against the United States and its allies. We are here to examine a vast spectrum of evidence about the motivations and consequences of the US invasion and occupation, evidence that has been deliberately marginalised or suppressed. Every aspect of the war will be examined – its legality, the role of international institutions and major corporations in the occupation, the role of the media, the impact of weapons such as depleted uranium munitions, napalm, and cluster bombs, the use of and legitimation of torture, the ecological impacts of the war, the responsibility of Arab governments, the impact of Iraq's occupation on Palestine, and the history of US and British military interventions in Iraq. This tribunal is an attempt to correct the record. To document the history of the war not from the point of view of the victors but of the temporarily – and I repeat the word temporarily – vanquished.

The writer Arundhati Roy, who opened the culminating session of the World Tribunal on Iraq, is the author of the prize-winning novel The God of Small Things.

Before the testimonies begin, I would like to briefly address as straightforwardly as I can a few questions that have been raised about this tribunal.

The first is that this tribunal is a Kangaroo Court. That it represents only one point of view. That it is a prosecution without a defence. That the verdict is a foregone conclusion. Now this view seems to suggest a touching concern that in this harsh world, the views of the US government and the so-called Coalition of the Willing headed by President George Bush and Prime Minister Tony Blair have somehow gone unrepresented. That the World Tribunal on Iraq isn't aware of the arguments in support of the war and is unwilling to consider the point of view of the invaders. If in the era of the multinational corporate media and embedded journalism anybody can seriously hold this view, then we truly do live in the Age of Irony, in an age when satire has become meaningless because real life is more satirical than satire can ever be.

Let me say categorically that this tribunal is the defence. It is an act of resistance in itself. It is a defence mounted against one of the most cowardly wars ever fought in history, a war in which international institutions were used to force a country to disarm and then stood by while it was attacked with a greater array of weapons than has ever been used in the history of war.

Second, this tribunal is not in any way a defence of Saddam Hussein. His crimes against Iraqis, Kurds, Iranians, Kuwaitis, and others cannot be written off in the process of bringing to light Iraq's more recent and still unfolding tragedy. However, we must not forget that when Saddam Hussein was committing his worst crimes, the US government was supporting him politically and materially. When he was gassing Kurdish people, the US government financed him, armed him, and stood by silently.

Saddam Hussein is being tried as a war criminal even as we speak. But what about those who helped to install him in power, who armed him, who supported him – and who are now setting up a tribunal to try him and absolve themselves completely? And what about other friends of the United States in the region that have suppressed Kurdish people's and other people's rights, including the government of Turkey?

There are remarkable people gathered here who in the face of this relentless and brutal aggression and propaganda have doggedly worked to compile a comprehensive spectrum of evidence and information that should serve as a weapon in the hands of those who wish to participate in the resistance against the occupation of Iraq. It should become a weapon in the hands of soldiers in the United States, the United Kingdom, Italy, Australia, and elsewhere who do not wish to fight, who do not wish to lay down their lives – or to take the lives of others – for a pack of lies. It should become a weapon in the hands of journalists, writers, poets, singers, teachers, plumbers, taxi drivers, car mechanics, painters, lawyers – anybody who wishes to participate in the resistance.

The evidence collated in this tribunal should, for instance, be used by the International Criminal Court (whose jurisdiction the United States does not recognise) to try as war criminals George Bush, Tony Blair, John Howard, Silvio

Berlusconi, and all those government officials, army generals, and corporate chief executives who participated in this war and now profit from it.

The assault on Iraq is an assault on all of us: on our dignity, our intelligence, and our future.

We recognise that the judgment of the World Tribunal on Iraq is not binding in international law. However, our ambitions far surpass that. The World Tribunal on Iraq places its faith in the consciences of millions of people across the world who do not wish to stand by and watch while the people of Iraq are being slaughtered, subjugated, and humiliated.

COMMUNICATION WORKERS UNION

End the Occupation of Iraq

Billy Hayes
General Secretary

Pat O'Hara
President

How the UN Failed Iraq

Hans von Sponeck

Hans von Sponeck served in the United Nations for 32 years, resigning his position as UN Humanitarian Coordinator in Iraq in protest at the impact of sanctions on the Iraqi people. He gave this assessment of the UN's role in relation to Iraq before and after the invasion in 2003 in Istanbul on the opening day of the World Tribunal on Iraq.

In discussing UN involvement before and after the 2003 invasion of United States, United Kingdom and other coalition forces into Iraq, a clear distinction has to be made between the policy makers and the civil servants expected to carry out the policies, i.e., between member governments in the UN Security Council and the UN Secretariat.

If this is done, it quickly becomes clear that primary responsibility for the human catastrophe in Iraq lies with the political UN, with those member governments in the UN Security Council who had the power to make a difference. The failure of the Council to make a humanitarian, ethical and legal difference is much more monumental than is commonly known. There is not only the betrayal of the Iraqi people but also the betrayal of the UN Charter and the betrayal of the international conscience.

Why is this so?

World leaders were hiding behind the curtain of the UN Security Council to premeditate their betrayal before and after the illegal war of 2003. There can be no more doubts; the facts are present, that the United States and United Kingdom governments were actively pursuing regime change by force at a time when the world was made to believe that international law, peaceful solutions to the conflict, and the protection of the Iraqi people were part of the US and UK governments' approach. They were not. Once the asymmetrical war was over, it also became clear to the international public that those who carried out this war had reached greater heights of irresponsibility by fighting this war without a strategy for peace.

The objective was to maintain a stranglehold on Iraq. Means of 'disarray' and 'deception' were deployed to justify the end of 'domination'. Iraq's armed forces were sent home. Civil servants were retired without evidence of wrongdoing, simply because they had belonged to the Ba'ath Party. New laws, the

Transition Authority laws (TAL) were introduced by decree. These laws tried to re-colonise Iraq economically and institutionally, and create dependence even in such areas as agriculture by banning local seed stocks in favour of genetically modified seeds to be imported from the United States. The ensuing Iraqi opposition and chaos left the occupying powers stymied and bewildered.

How did the UN Security Council and the UN Secretariat react to these bilateral aberrations?

Over a decade, the UN Security Council condoned what two permanent members, the United States and the United Kingdom, were doing to pursue, first, their Iraq containment policy and later their regime replacement agenda. This amounted to nothing less than the *de facto* bilateralisation of the Security Council. The rhetoric of the Iraq debates in the Council showed that there was an abundance of awareness of the evolving humanitarian crisis in Iraq. At the same time there was a severe shortage of political will to take timely steps to redress this situation.

It was known to all members of the Security Council that the linkage between disarmament and comprehensive economic sanctions meant that the people of Iraq were made to pay a heavy price in terms of life and destitution for acts of their government. It was known to all members of the Security Council that the inadequacy of the Council's allocations for the oil-for-food programme, and the bureaucracy with which this humanitarian exemption was implemented, worsened the chances of survival of many Iraqis. It was known to all members of the Security Council that the refusal by the Council to allow the transfer of cash to Iraq's central bank needed to run the nation, to pay for training, installation of equipment and institution building, encouraged the Government of Iraq to increase illegal means to obtain cash.

It was known to all members of the Security Council that the establishment of the two no-fly-zones within Iraq had little to do with the protection of ethnic and religious groups but a lot to do with destabilisation. All members of the Security Council were aware that, following 'Operation Desert Fox' in December 1998, the US and the UK governments, having given their pilots broader rules of engagement, used Iraqi airspace as a training ground, eventually in preparation for war. The Security Council had access to air strike reports when such reports were prepared by the UN in Baghdad, and therefore all members of the Security Council knew of the destruction of civilian life and property. Yet, the Security Council never debated the legality of the no-fly-zones, to challenge two of its members that they maintained these zones without a UN mandate.

All this was known.

With rare exceptions, members of the Security Council allowed the Council to become a convenient tool for the pursuit of bilateral policies. There was ample experience in the Council concerning the danger of misuse of consensus resolutions, as demonstrated by the handling of resolutions 687 (1991) and 1284 (1999) by the United States and the United Kingdom governments. This did not deter members of the Council from going along with yet another consensus resolution, 1441 (2002). The likelihood of misuse by individual members of the

Council of provisions such as 'material breaches' and 'serious consequences' to justify military invasion should have prevented the adoption of such a resolution.

The UN Secretariat acquiesced when the United States and United Kingdom, two founding members of the United Nations, insisted in the Security Council on an economic sanctions regime that caused a human tragedy. The UN Secretariat remained mute when these same governments dropped out of the international community to unilaterally mount an illegal invasion of Iraq. The UN Secretariat did not react even at this critical time when the very foundation of the institution was threatened. Dr. Hans Blix, chief UN arms inspector, had reported progress in verifying Iraq's lack of weapons of mass destruction, and was pleading for more time to complete the inspection process. The UN Secretariat should have used this to confront the two governments about their war plans, but chose not to do so. Without protest, the UN Secretariat withdrew the UN arms inspectors in March 2003.

The UN Secretariat could not have prevented the long planned decision to go to war. The sheer seriousness of the violation of international law by two member countries, and the sidelining of a world body created to prevent wars, represented a challenge for the UN civil service to show that, ultimately, conscience was superior to obedience.

Since the illegal invasion of Iraq, there has not been a debate in the Security Council about the fundamental disregard by the coalition forces of existing conventions created to ensure that the occupation armies act in accordance with the Hague and Geneva Conventions to which they are parties. Looting and burning of the national museum and the national library, the damaging of archaeological sites, and the humiliating treatment of civilians by the US armed forces, provoked no protest in the Security Council. The Security Council watched impotently when the soul and ethos of Iraq was attacked. The detention of political figures for indefinite periods, and the unimaginable brutality and sadism with which detainees were treated not just in Abu Ghraib and Camp Bucca, but also in other prisons were not the subject of Security Council concern. Wholesale destruction of towns such as Al Fallujah, Tel Afar and Al Qaim did not ruffle the Security Council and lead to emergency meetings. There were no protests in the Council that Coalition Provisional Authority administrator Paul Bremer and other CPA officials represented an allegedly liberated and sovereign Iraq at major international meetings such as the World Economic Forum in Amman, and the World Trade Organisation in Geneva. The Security Council took no note of the fact that the assignment of a human rights rapporteur for Iraq was abruptly terminated by the UN Human Rights Commission in Geneva following the illegal war. The Security Council agreed in 2003 to the continuation of payments by the UN Compensation Commission even though it had earlier agreed to discontinue the entertainment of claims.

The Security Council did play an important role in the preparations for an interim Iraqi administration and elections, but ultimately succumbed to US heavy handedness in deciding the details of the process.

In the history books of the United Nations, the handling of the Iraq conflict by the Security Council will be recorded as a massive failure of oversight responsibility.

The history books should also record that the voice of the people replaced the UN Security Council as the international conscience. This voice must not relent in its demands that the United States and United Kingdom Governments, bilaterally, as national administrations, and multilaterally, as permanent members of the UN Security Council, are accountable to their people and to the world community for their wrongdoing against Iraq, before, during and after the illegal war.

It is a crime in many countries to leave the scene of an accident without helping the victims. This also applies to the responsibility of the international community to help the Iraqi victims. Conscience, compassion, and a sense of responsibility are powerful reasons to stay involved. There must be involvement at two levels: Iraq and United Nations reforms.

Political leaders urge that we should look forward. This we must. However, a look forward receives legitimacy only when it is linked to accountability for the past. This applies to nations, communities, individuals – to everyone, particularly to those in power. The forthcoming trial of Iraq's former President Saddam Hussein acknowledges his accountability for past crimes against his people. The same applies to crimes against humanity committed by those who maintained economic sanctions with total disregard for the human costs, who fought a silent war in the no-fly-zones, who invaded Iraq, who abused, maimed, tortured and killed its people. The dock of the court-room for Iraq has to have more than one chair! Law and justice, need it be stressed, are not only for the losers.

There are thousands of unnamed Iraqi fathers, mothers and children who are victims of the failure to prevent war and destruction in Iraq. Let them be the stark reminders of our responsibility to keep the debate alive at least until the terms of accountability are met.

In summary, Iraq remains 'unfinished business' for the international peace movement and responsible citizens everywhere. The challenge is to address three major issues:

1. The United Nations has failed in preventing unjust economic sanctions, an illegal war, and carnage under occupation.

This means that in the short term, the peace movement must persevere in its demands that those responsible be brought to justice. It must not be forgotten that what was done in the name of 'freedom', 'democracy' and 'human rights' represents a travesty of the meaning of 'freedom', 'democracy' and 'human rights'.

In the medium term, the peace movement must forcefully contribute to the debate on UN reforms to create a structure which is protected against misuse. This involves much more than the enlargement of the Security Council.

2. The international peace movement, too, has failed in preventing unjust economic sanctions and an illegal war.

In the short term, the peace movement should take this as an important opportunity to carry out a self-critical review why this failure occurred and what factors contributed to this failure.

The dangers looming on the political and socio-economic horizon are horrific. The reaction of the peace movement, in the medium term, must be to leave turf battles and institutional or personal ambitions behind, to facilitate significantly better organised responses to international crises. Only combined commitment and a joint strategy offer a chance to make a difference.

3. As individuals who understand and cherish the ethos of the UN Charter, who believe in peace and justice for all, who are abhorred by what has happened in Iraq before, during and after the illegal war, we must first and foremost work on ourselves to become equipped for the tasks ahead. Beyond this obligation, we have to remain, in the words of Dag Hammarskjoeld, the UN's second secretary general, 'conscious of the reality of evil and the tragedy of individual life, and conscious, too, of the demand that life be conducted with decency.'

Albert Einstein, Bertrand Russell, Manifesto 50
The Spokesman - 85
Edited by Ken Coates
Requiem - **Kurt Vonnegut**
Building the Bomb
Michele Ernsting, Joseph Rotblat & Ken Coates
The Russell-Einstein Manifesto 50 Years On
Bertrand Russell & Albert Einstein
Convert & Disarm - **Seymour Melman**
The First Fireball - **John Berger**
Doctrines & Visions - **Noam Chomsky**
Bring the Troops Home - **Edward Kennedy**

Single issue £5 plus £1 postage. One year's subscription to *The Spokesman*
(4 issues) costs £20 (£25, €40/$40 ex UK) Credit/Debit cards accepted
Spokesman Books Russell House, Bulwell Lane, Nottingham, NG6 0BT, England
Tel: 0115 9708318 | **e-mail:** elfeuro@compuserve.com
www.spokesmanbooks.com

Unfinished Business for the Peace Movement

Ken Coates

Ken Coates contributed this paper for the closing session of the Istanbul Tribunal.

Our people need to know what has been happening in Iraq: but a systematic analysis of the terrible events there is necessary for more reasons than those of public instruction. Unless we learn from these events they will be repeated: and the signs are that the repetitions could be soon. In a word, the detailed examination of the war in Iraq is important throughout the world, and above all to peace movements because of the light it throws on military intentions, on the balance of military power, and on overall threats to the peace of the world.[1]

I

Like the Generals who always get ready to fight the last war, peace movements do tend to be dominated by the thinking of a previous generation of strategists. They have more excuse than the Generals, because they are not normally privy to what Generals know about the state of the world, and the nature of power. They do also tend to be more innocent. However, to paraphrase Donald Rumsfeld, not the least consequence of the war in Iraq has been that many things that were previously unknown are now known.

For a very long time peace activists have been left to pick the bones out of the remnants of the Cold War. We have not been very good at that. In the 1980s, campaigners for European Nuclear Disarmament called for the simultaneous dissolution of the great nuclear alliances, Nato and the Warsaw Treaty Organisation. Following the rise of Gorbachev, the Warsaw Treaty quickly fell apart, but Nato, after a very momentary quiescence, simply grew and grew, until it directly embraced large numbers of territories in Eastern Europe, and indirectly entered formal 'partnerships for peace' with large parts of the former Soviet Union. The peace movements, to give them their due, were uneasy about this expansion, but they were quite unable to stop it. By March

2004 Bulgaria, Romania, Slovakia and Slovenia all became full Nato members. The Czech Republic, Hungary and Poland had joined five years earlier, in March 1999. Three countries which are now independent, but were formerly constituent parts of the Soviet Union: Estonia, Latvia and Lithuania, also enrolled themselves on the 29th March 2004. Other accessions are undoubtedly slated.

In the years of this transition, numerous conflicts were seeded, which even divided the peace movements, as happened in Yugoslavia and Afghanistan. It has taken some time, and a number of alarming developments in weapons systems and nuclear military technology, to give rise again to a halting renaissance of the demand for the removal of all nuclear weapons from the area of Europe.

Of course, the fundamental result of the end of the Cold War, has been ending of bipolar conflict and the emergence of a single dominant megapower.[2] The American military quickly codified the new balance by developing the new doctrine of Full Spectrum Dominance. This is proclaimed to be:

'The ability of US forces, operating unilaterally or in combination with multinational and interagency partners, to defeat any adversary and control any situation across the full range of military operations ... It includes theatre engagement and presence activities. It includes conflict involving employment of strategic forces and weapons of mass destruction, major theatre wars, regional conflicts, and smaller-scale contingencies. [It implies] freedom to operate in all domains – space, sea, land, air and information.'

As with many doctrines, there is more than one slip betwixt cup and lip. It is easy to proclaim military supremacy, but can be more difficult to secure it. However, even before the new doctrine, the United States had indeed already enjoyed long years of military invulnerability. Nobody has been or is in a position to invade the country even without the best efforts of the military industrial complex: there are no land forces able to assault the United States from Mexico, or Canada, and all Latin America is comparatively weak and poor, seriously divided, and largely introspective. At the same time, there is wider dominance. The United States has an impressive control of the seas. Britain certainly does not rule the waves any more, and has sublet its remaining outposts of naval power to the United States. Notably, Diego Garcia has been illegally expropriated by the British for the benefit of the American air force, and to the immense detriment of America's chosen enemies in the Middle East and Africa.

All this concerns only conventional domination, long since surpassed. *Joint Vision 20/10* proclaims a coming bonfire of the Treaties, because

'the medium of space is the fourth medium of warfare – along with land, sea and air. Space power (systems capabilities and forces) will be increasingly leveraged to close the ever-widening gap between diminishing resources and increasing military commitments.'

And, in case we were in any doubt, 'information superiority relies heavily upon space capabilities'.

With such unchallengeable ascendancy in arms, it is hardly surprising that America has effortlessly sought to rig the balance of power in Eurasia to its advantage. Hence, formerly Soviet oil courses from Azerbaijan across Georgia into Turkey and thus the Mediterranean. American bases are scattered across former Soviet Central Asia so that Nato cannot today criticise the repression in Uzbekistan for fear of annoying American clients in that country. There is really a vast accumulation of force and potential force, enough to daunt all conventional military rivals.

And yet, in the attacks of Al Qaeda, a handful of people employing weapons no more deadly than Stanley knives, were able to mount a destructive foray against New York, destroying the Twin Towers of the World Trade Centre. This was not, contrary to official propaganda, the opening of a war. There was no warring power capable of concluding such a war. Legally the atrocity of 9/11 fell under the criminal law, and this appreciation was at least partially refracted in the subsequent decision of the American Government that its 'war' on terrorism did not fall within the provisions of the Geneva Conventions.

Once again, international law has been rewritten by the marshals, who routinely annul all lingering notions of right or justice. These processes have been at work on a larger stage.[3]

II

Of course the United Nations was the creation of the wartime alliance against Hitler's Germany and the axis powers. Its founding conference in San Francisco took place at a time when the Alliance had never been stronger, and would never be closer. The Charter of the new organisation was carefully sculpted to maintain the unity of the wartime alliance, and to safeguard the rights of its principal contenders. The veto, or rule of unanimity, assured that the five great powers in the alliance: USA, the USSR, Britain, France and China, would never have their vital interests violated by any decision of the new body. This prudent precaution soon gained an altogether new meaning, as the alliance fractured into the Cold War, which more than once ran the risk of becoming hot.

Viewed in retrospect, the more than half-century of the UN's history is a remarkable achievement. Those who designed this structure had learnt well from the difficult story of the League of Nations, which proved much more vulnerable to events in the interwar years than did the UN in the seismic period of the nuclear arms race. Certainly the nature of this threat did, in itself, contribute to the will to maintain a viable international organisation.

Now the need for the reform of this organisation has been widely accepted, and has generated an official report by the High-level Panel on Threats, Challenges and Change, set up by the Secretary General. Reform, however, is not so easy. Much argument has been lavished on the injustices of the veto. For the great powers, the objection is usually to other people's vetoes.

There is a special problem which attaches to the maintenance of a United Nations Organisation, when one nation has unchallenged pre-eminence over all the others. As Jack Straw, the British Foreign Secretary argued, when seeking to persuade the British Parliament that they dare not defy American wishes and refuse the war in Iraq:

'... you are right it is the United States which has the military power to act as the world's policeman, and only the United States. We live in a uni-polar world; the United States has a quarter of the world's wealth, the world's GDP, and it has stronger armed forces than the next 27 countries put together. So its predominance is huge. That is a fact. No one can gainsay it; no one can change it in the short or medium term. The choice we have to make in the international community is whether, in a uni-polar world, we want the only superpower to act unilaterally and we force them to act unilaterally or whether we work in such a way that they act within the multilateral institutions. What I say to France and Germany and all other European Union colleagues is to take care, because just as America helps to define and influence our politics, so what we do in Europe helps to define and influence American politics. We will reap a whirlwind if we push the Americans into a unilateralist position in which they are the centre of this uni-polar world.'

But undoubtedly the foundation of the UN rested on the appreciation, derived from Immanuel Kant, that the foundations of the international order rested on Nation States. A State is a society of human beings, Kant taught, that no one other than itself can command or dispose of. The collaboration of such States depended on the appreciation that each was, in truth, inviolable. As Kant himself said in his proposal to secure perpetual peace, 'No State shall forcibly interfere in the constitution and government of another State'. 'Limited' sovereignty, or the doctrine that 'sovereignty is less absolute than in earlier times' would sap the fundamental agreement on which the United Nations rests, which is why Kofi Annan, no firebrand, nonetheless insisted that the war on Iraq was illegal, insofar as it was undertaken without either direct justification in self-defence, or the mandate of the Security Council of the UN.

Surely the modern world has moved beyond the age of Kant? The answer has to be yes, and no. If political economy is the true foundation of civil society, then globalisation is assuredly eroding the powers of nations. There are also more beneficial pressures which enlarge the co-operation between the institutions of civil society across frontiers. But civil society has certainly not attained a fully integrated global presence.

The word of Amnesty International resounds around the world but the limitations of the influence of that organisation are all-too evident. Kant thought that if reforming States could aspire to similar 'republican' governments, they could then federate in a League of Nations which 'need not be a state of Nations'. But similar and parallel evolution of institutions is only the beginning of a very long march to the integration of civil society across national frontiers.

For a time, it looked as if the European Union could fulfil the dreams not only of Kant, but also of Tom Paine and William Penn, growing into 'an ever closer union'. We may well think that links between peace movements, and wider common actions between voluntary bodies are the groundwork upon which another world becomes possible. But this does not imply that we can simply jump over the inherited institutions. These institutions have nuclear teeth, and their military rationality remains untamed, even if a new, more humane rationality is slowly evolving among the peoples.

We tried to build the Russell Tribunals on war crimes in Vietnam and on repression in Latin America, on this foundation. In the words of Lelio Basso, the Tribunals became necessary because 'human rights are at the same time proclaimed and left unprotected, devoid of international or national safeguards'.

It is clear that the problems have all been aggravated since those days: but the war in Iraq shows with fierce cruelty how little progress we have made in our institutional responses to those problems.

Today we see in the flood of embarrassing documents on the true origins of the Iraq war, a fierce tension between the constitutional foundations of the UN, and the real power relationships. The United States believes that it exercises 'Full Spectrum Dominance' in military terms, and that it does not need any permissions to assert its will wherever it feels the need to do so. Why else expend all that treasure, all those efforts to create an armed power beyond compare, if it is to generate no dividends in actual behaviour? But it takes two to tango, as was seen in the case of Turkey, not the strongest member of the North Atlantic Alliance, who refused to fall in behind George Bush and Jack Straw in declaring war on Iraq.

The culmination of the recent revelations was perhaps the publication on May 1st in the Sunday Times of London of the so-called Downing Street memo, now generally described in the United States as Downing Streetgate.[4]

A spate of leaks of classified memoranda shows that British officials in Washington believed in July 2002 that 'war was inevitable', and that 'the intelligence and facts were being fixed around the policy'. These documents have provoked sustained enquiries in the United States, and a powerful campaign by Representative John Conyers Jnr. They show us the sense in which it is true that domination is not enough. American satellites could pinpoint every movement in the Iraqi desert, but could not control the growing apprehensions of public opinion around the world.

It was presumed that those things which could not be accomplished by military gadgetry might be brought about by the expenditure of money. But astonishingly bribery was not a sufficient weapon to bring the Security Council of the United Nations on side with the projected war. These intransigent facts could not stop the war, and the slaughter of at least one hundred thousand Iraqi civilians. But they could deny that war legitimacy, and thus establish a large space in which the movement for peace and human rights can develop.

This will require a hard-headed appreciation of the scope and limitations of agreements between nations, and their institutional arrangements. In defending the United Nations, we are defending not what has been passed down to us, a long history of shabby compromises, but a continuous space for co-operation and democracy, a Commonwealth that is to come. When the British working people demanded the extension of the franchise, they were not seeking to consummate the somewhat raddled history of the mother of Parliaments: rather they were struggling to pass beyond the old corruption, into a new and better world. Another world is, truly, possible.[5]

Footnotes

1. To follow the attempt to develop the work of the World Tribunal on Iraq, please go to www.worldtribunal.org.
2. Various campaigns have devoted their efforts to tracing and documenting the consequences of this development. The surge in military preparations is highlighted in the development of nuclear weaponry, and the evolution of advanced plans to site offensive weapons in space. The campaign against Star Wars can be visited at www.space4peace.org.

   The extensive spawning of military bases by the United States now spreads all around the world, and includes numerous emplacements in the territories of States belonging to the former Soviet Union. (http://lists.riseup.net/www/info/nousbases)
3. The war on terror has produced a whole series of setbacks for human rights, although real terrorists, we are told, have done nothing but thrive since the occupation of Iraq. Civil liberties have not been so fortunate. This problem will be one of the themes of the next meeting of the Bertrand Russell Network for Peace and Human Rights, in Brussels on October 20th and 21st 2005. More information can be found at www.russfound.org, and also at www.statewatch.org.
4. See the remarkable series of leaked documents which reveal the advice given to Tony Blair by his officials, during the covert preparations for the coming war on Iraq. (www.afterdowningstreet.org)
5. Go to www.forumsocialmundial.org.br. The campaign for the removal of American nuclear weapons from Europe can be found at www.abolition2000europe.org. The overall campaign against new nuclear weapons in the context of the failure of the Review Conference of the Non-proliferation Treaty is at www.acronym.org.

No More Hiroshimas
Poems & translations by James Kirkup

It is 60 years since the atomic bombing of Hiroshima and Nagasaki. These events inspired *No More Hiroshimas*, a collection of poems by the distinguished poet James Kirkup, which is belatedly published for the first time in Britain.

'These poems all have their roots in one late afternoon at the land workers' hostel outside Ponteland, Northumberland… As we entered the hostel we got the news that the first American Atom Bomb had been dropped on Japan, on the city of Hiroshima. It was the first time we had heard of that place that was to become auniversal symbol of man's inhumanity towards his fellow-men' **James Kirkup**

$12/€12/£6.99 | ISBN 0 85124 689 3 | 72pp

www.spokesmanbooks.com
email: elfeuro@compuserve.com
credit/debit cards welcome -

Available from **Spokesman Books**
Russell House, Bulwell Lane, Nottingham,
NG6 0BT England | **Tel:** 0115 9708318

Philosophical Arabesques

Nikolai Bukharin

Nikolai Bukharin was one of the most talented leaders of the Russian Revolution of 1917, and a member of the Soviet government. He was eventually imprisoned by Stalin for treason.

Philosophical Arabesques, written in the Lubyanka Prison in Moscow, is the most important of his prison writings.

The book defends the genuine legacy of Lenin's Marxism against the use of his memory to legitimise totalitarian power.

In its pages, Bukharin covers the full range of issues in Marxist philosophy – the sources of knowledge, the nature of truth, freedom and necessity, the relationship between Hegelian and Marxist dialectics.

Consigned to the Kremlin archives for a half-century after Bukharin's execution, this work is now being published for the first time in English. It is an essential reference work for scholars of Marxism and the Russian revolution and a landmark in the history of prison writing.

- **Beautiful hardback edition published in August 2005**
- **Advance orders available from Pluto Press at www.plutobooks.com or phone our warehouse on 01264 342 832**

Published by Pluto Press • August 2005 • Hb • £35.00 • 0745324770

Independent Progressive Publishing
www.plutobooks.com

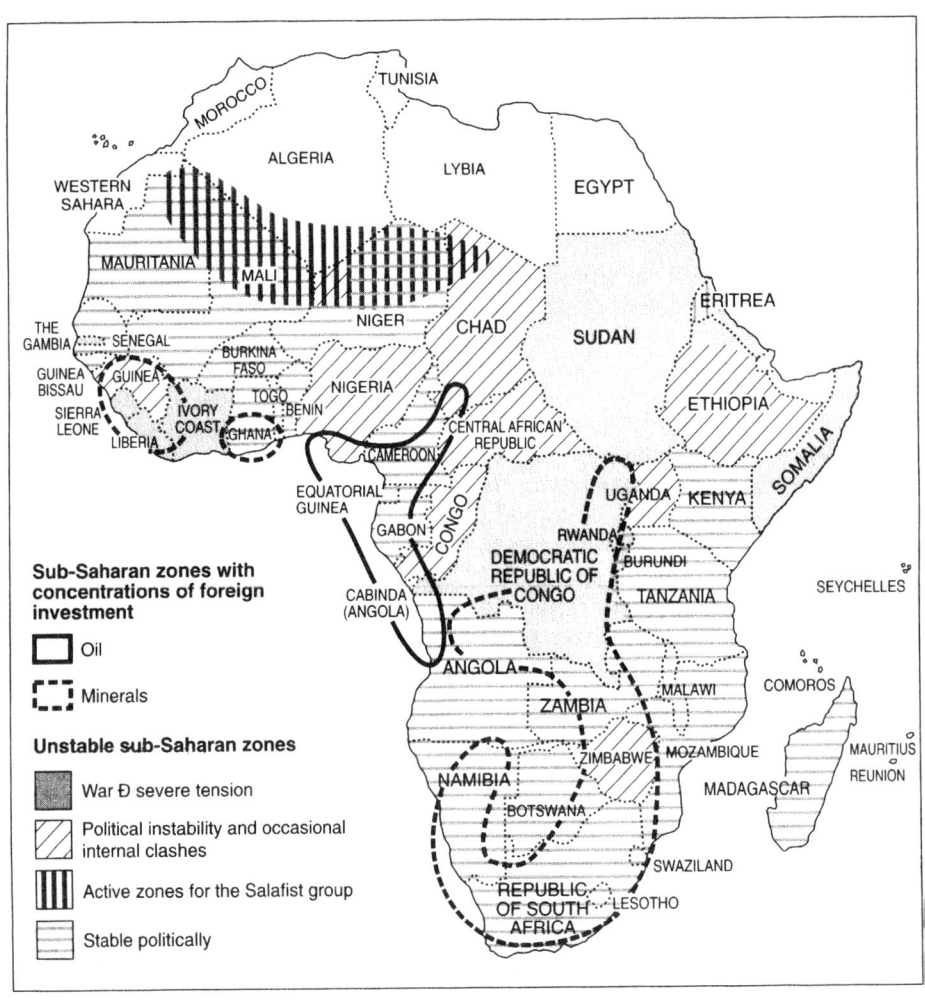

Source: Pierre Abramovici, *Le Monde Diplomatique,* reproduced in *Review of African Political Economy,* no 102, 2004, page 687.

Mr Blair's Africa

Michael Barratt Brown

Michael Barratt Brown is the author of Africa's Choices, After Imperialism, *and* Global Crisis: A Young Person's Guide *(Spokesman Books £9).*

In 2004, Mr. Blair decided in the context of Britain's G(Great Power)8 and European Union Presidency in 2005, to set up a Commission for Africa. 'Africa', he said, 'is a scar on the conscience of the world', and appealed to his Christian commitment as guarantee of sincerity in his concern for the failure of Africa to keep up with the rising standard of living in the rest of the world. Gordon Brown, who has shown a continuing interest in alleviating Africa's debt burden, was not to be upstaged in an Election year, and set off on a tour of African states. But it appears from the statements which Blair has made at subsequent conferences in Africa that he, and probably Brown, too, have another agenda besides that of humanitarian aid:

> 'even before September 11, Al Qaeda had bases in Africa. They still do. Hiding in places where they can go undisturbed by weak governments, where they can plan their next attack, which could be anywhere in the world.' (Tony Blair, Conference on African Development, Addis Ababa, 07.10.04)

Taking this interest in what have come to be called 'the failed states of Africa', Mr. Blair is but following his American masters, whose military interest in North and West Africa has been growing rapidly in recent years:

> 'We have said for a long time that if you squeeze the terrorists in Afghanistan, Pakistan, Iraq and other places, they will find new places and one of those places is the Sahel/Maghreb' (Colonel Victor Nelson, responsible for the Pan-Sahel Initiative to US Air Force Maj. Gen. Jeff Kohler, director of European Command's Plans and Policy Division)

This Sahel-Maghreb covers a large part of Africa – all of North Africa and the region south of the Sahara. It is true that there are 'failed states' in this region and that the region includes some with the very lowest living standards. But some are at the same time oil states, in which US, British and French interests are particularly strong. To decide about the relative importance of Mr Blair's two sets of agenda, it is necessary, first, to discover the causes of the poverty and the failure of the 'failed states' and, second, to question how serious is the threat of 'terrorism' and what else might be the reason for Western military interest in Africa.

The origins of political and economic failure in Africa

There is no doubt about Africa's backwardness. Blair's description of it, in announcing the Africa Commission in February 2004, was only too accurate:

> 'Africa is the only continent to have grown poorer in the past 25 years, its share of world trade has halved in the generation, and it receives less than 1% of direct foreign investment, 44 million children do not go to school, millions, as you know, die through famine, or disease, or conflict, and Africa risks being left even further behind.'

But what is the cause of this disaster? Most African peoples had been under European colonial rule for nearly two centuries until the 1950s, and were liberated in the form of over 50 separate nation states. Apart from Egypt, Nigeria and South Africa none of these has a population large enough to provide markets for economies of scale in industrial development. Yet the African states have perpetuated the colonial territorial divisions, which often separated ethnic groupings, and the élites which inherited power have been encouraged to preserve these divisions by the international institutions – the International Monetary Fund and World Bank in particular. Attempts have been made to form united African organisations and regional groupings, but with little success because of the ties which the Afican élites retained with their erstwhile colonial rulers. The reason for this continuation was to exercise control over the two or three commodities whose production the colonial powers had developed in each colony, whether it was coffee, tea, cocoa, tobacco, sugar, timber, rubber, copper, iron, gold or diamonds, to which list oil has subsequently been added.

It is the members of these élite groups, which inherited power from their erstwhile colonial rulers, and of the succeeding élites, who are pilloried now for corruption and weak governance. But these are élites which were the product of colonial rule, either invented tribal chiefs to act as indirect rulers (see Terence Ranger 'The Invention of Tradition in Colonial Africa' in Eric Hobsbawm and Terence Ranger, *The Invention of Tradition*, Cambridge University Press, 1983), or employed as traders with the Europeans, first organising the supply of slaves and then centrally involved in the trade in colonial commodities. They replaced the many forms of indigenous African government, whose history was deliberately wiped out by the Colonial Powers, leaving behind a tragic lack of institutional capacity and human self-confidence, when the day of liberation dawned.

For two decades after liberation the successor states in Africa benefited from their rich resources, and their economies grew, but with little diversification from the colonial pattern of production for export, except that oil was added to the list. Then commodity prices began to fall. Oil was the exception, but this only meant that the non-oil producing countries ran up debts to pay for higher priced oil while the world prices of other commodities fell and at the same time interest rates were raised world wide. By the 1990s, for every dollar of aid supplied by the rich industrialised countries to Africa 80 cents was returning in debt repayment. The reasons for the fall in commodity prices were several: extra incomes in the rich countries were being spent on services and not on goods; less material was being used in manufacturing processes; artificial substitutes such as nylon and plastics were replacing natural materials; and to cap all this, indebted producing countries were being encouraged by the financial institutions – the IMF and World Bank – to increase production for export to pay off their debts, leading to overproduction and still further falling prices. Africa's share in world trade has fallen and investment in Africa has fallen because world trade in commodities has not kept up with world trade in manufactures.

The difficulties facing primary commodity producers in Africa were further compounded by their increased exploitation at the hands of the ruling élites seeking to make up for falling world prices. To obtain further loans, indebted African governments agreed with the financial institutions to structural adjustment programmes (SAPs) which involved reducing public spending and opening their borders to imported products from the industrialised countries. This even came to include cereals whose export was subsidised in the rich countries so that poor country producers who could not compete on price lost business. As public spending was cut back, the whole basis of government shrank and élites became dependent not on taxes and local revenues but increasingly on direct control over the chief commodities exported from their country, and on corrupt payments and arms supplied from the outside companies trading these commodities. It is this corruption involving a flight of capital, as increasing sums were invested outside Africa because of the historic disbelief in the capacity for local development, that is said to typify African government, and that Mr Blair has promised to challenge. But, as is becomingly widely recognised, for every person corrupted there must be a corruptor, and this is generally not an African.

One example will serve to illustrate what has been happening. It comes from Liberia, as its name implies, settled originally by freed slaves. Liberia is typical of the 'failed states', having had virtually no government for the last two decades, but with historically important exports of iron ore, rubber and timber controlled by foreign companies, including Firestone Rubber. Until the end of the Cold War Liberia received large funds from United States aid which were used by a certain Samuel Doe to maintain his security and patronage networks. When these funds ceased, several groups took up arms against the state, including one group led by Charles Taylor, who after protracted civil war established himself as President. Most of the big foreign companies such as Firestone left as the war hotted up, but a number of smaller firms, and at least one large firm, the Malaysia based Oriental Timber Corporation in the timber industry, remained with important markets in France and China. These firms allegedly supplied Taylor with funds for his police and private militia. Although the war is now ended and Taylor exiled to Nigeria,

> ## Africa opened for business
> Multinational corporations have been given control of the primary instrument of US policy towards Africa, the African Growth and Opportunity Act. To become eligible for help, African countries must bring about 'a market-based economy that protects private property rights', 'the elimination of barriers to United States trade and investment' and a conducive environment for US 'foreign policy interests'. In return they will be allowed 'preferential treatment' for some of their products in US markets.
>
> Clothing factories in Africa will be allowed to sell their products to the US as long as they use 'fabrics wholly formed and cut in the United States' or if they avoid direct competition with US products. All this is classified as foreign aid. The act instructs the US Agency for International Development to develop 'a receptive environment for trade and investment'. Its implementation has been outsourced to the Corporate Council on Africa.
>
> The Council is the lobby group representing the big US corporations with interests in Africa: Halliburton, Exxon Mobil, Coca-Cola, General Motors, Starbucks, Raytheon, Microsoft, Boeing, Cargill, Citigroup and others. 'Until African countries are able to earn greater income,' says the Council, 'their

Liberian state institutions barely exist. No statistics for Liberia appear in international publications. Tens of thousands of families fled to neighbouring countries, but timber, often illegally logged without environmental concern and with Malaysian labour, continues to be exported. (For this story I am indebted to Patrick Johnston of the NW University, Illinois 'Timber Booms, State Busts: The Political Economy of Liberian Timber', *Review of African Political Economy*, no 101, 2004).

A roughly similar story can be told of the war in Sierra Leone for control over diamond exports, and of the continuing war in the copper rich Democratic Republic of Congo. In the Congo, which for a time came to be called Zaire, the liberation hero Patrice Lumumba was murdered by outside intervention and replaced by a US nominee, Mobutu Sese Seko. Mobutu ran his government entirely by patronage and made himself a billionaire from his share of the export earnings of the copper companies, but left his country with an external debt that was twice the value of the national product (see M. Barratt Brown, *Africa's Choices*, Penguin 1995, pp.306-7).

The discovery of oil in Africa, far from bringing peace and prosperity to the region, has only proliferated the number of states where power is fought for by two or more small local élites, supported and armed by one or more of the giant international oil companies and their national governments. Violence in the Niger Delta oil fields illustrates the problems arising from the fact that power in African governments is not based on local revenues but on control of natural resources

...bility to buy US products will be limited.' The US state department has put ... in charge of training African governments and businesses. It runs the US ...overnment's annual forum for African business, and hosts the Growth and ...pportunity Act's steering committee.

Something similar is being set up in the United Kingdom. The Business ...ction for Africa summit met in London in July as the G8 leaders gathered ... Scotland. Chaired by Sir Mark Moody-Stuart, the head of Anglo American, ...s speakers included executives from Shell, British American Tobacco, ...tandard Chartered Bank, De Beers and the Corporate Council on Africa. It ...augurated the Investment Climate Facility, a $550m fund financed by the ...K's foreign-aid budget, the World Bank and the other G8 nations, but ...riven and controlled by the private sector'. The fund will be launched by ...iall FitzGerald, now head of Reuters, but formerly chief executive of ...nilever. He wants the facility, he says, to help create a 'healthy investment ...imate' that will offer companies 'attractive financial returns compared to ...ompeting destinations'. Anglo American and Barclays have already ...olunteered to help.

With acknowledgements to George Monbiot, The Guardian

linked to giant foreign companies – in the case of Nigeria chiefly Shell and Chevron-Texaco. Decentralisation of power from the federal centre to local states – 36 in today's Nigeria – only exacerbates the competition among élites, which is not assuaged by forms of Community Partnership such as Shell has adopted (see Anna Zalik, 'The Niger Delta: "Petro Violence" and "Partnership Development"', *Review of African Political Economy*, September 2004, no. 101, vol. 31). The successive government coups in Africa's oil states bear terrible witness to this unholy alliance of local élites and foreign oil companies.

British and US military interest in Africa – terrorists or oil?

There is no doubt that much of the new British and US interest in Africa has a military involvement, not only in civil wars, as in the case of the British involvement in Sierra Leone, about which Mr. Blair has expressed much self-satisfaction, but also in the Maghreb-Sahel, in the Gulf of Guinea, and along the Red Sea. It is to be noted that this is where the oil is, but the explanation given by Mr. Blair and by the US military is that the threat in these regions is from terrorists. It is certainly true that Al Qaeda did once have its headquarters in Sudan and claimed responsibility for the bombing of the US embassies in Nairobi and Dar Es Salaam in 1998, but the American assertion that there is a major terrorist threat in Algeria and the Sahel has been questioned. Jeremy Keenan of the University of East Anglia has published a series of articles in the *Review of African Political Economy* (Nos. 99, 101 and 102 on 'Terror in the Sahara: the

Implications of US Imperialism for North and West Africa'). These all suggest that US and Algerian intelligence services have been fabricating, or at least greatly exaggerating, stories of terrorist activity in the region, in order to justify US military involvement. There is certainly drug smuggling across the Sahara, but a more important consideration must be the oil and gas in Algeria, Chad, and Nigeria, and all down along the Gulf of Guinea.

Mr Blair's speech to the Labour Party Conference in 2001, just after 9/11, played on the threat to British security as coming not just from Al Qaeda but much more widely. As he turned to the former Yugoslavia, to Rwanda, Sierra Leone, the Democratic Republic of the Congo (DRC), Zimbabwe and 'the state of Africa', in all these areas Blair saw the need for 'reasoned intervention' of Britain and the 'world community'. This is what Robert Cooper, a senior Blair advisor, has called with patronising arrogance 'the new liberal – and voluntary – imperialism… where the efficient and well-governed export stability and liberty' to evidently welcoming poor and failed states (*The Observer* World View Extra, 07.04.02). Security and a better life for Africans is being sold by Blair as ensuring more security for British people. Jack Straw spelled out his leader's concern, devoting an entire speech in 2002 to Africa. As the anniversary of 9/11 came round he argued that those dreadful events:

> 'give us a vision of one possible future – a future in which unspeakable acts of evil are committed against us, coordinated from failed states in distant parts of the world.'

Straw, speaking as Foreign Secretary, then went on to refer specifically to Somalia, Liberia, and the Democratic Republic of the Congo, linking these 'failed states' directly to British social problems and national security:

> 'as well as bringing mass murder to the heart of Manhattan, state failure has brought terror and misery to swathes of the African continent, as it did to the Balkans in the early 1990s, and at home has brought drugs, violence and crime to Britain's streets'.

These are only words, but about the military activity there can be no doubt in fact. An article in *Le Monde Diplomatique* by Pierre Abramovici in 2004, reproduced in *Review of African Political Economy* (no. 102, 2004) entitled 'United States: New Scramble for Africa', was noted in an earlier edition of *The Spokesman* (no. 83 in 2004). This article spelled out the increasing US military activity, with British support in some cases, taking place in Africa. As part of the American Pan Sahel Initiative (PSI), military assistance was supplied from November 2003 to help Mali, Chad, Niger and Mauritania (notably weak states with dictatorial rulers) to combat smuggling and terrorism, with US troops and equipment assembled at RAF bases in Britain. The following March 23-24 the chiefs of staff of Chad, Mali, Mauritania, Morocco, Niger, Senegal and Tunisia met at the US army's European Command (US-EUCOM) HQ in Stuttgart to discuss anti-terrorist operations in the Sahel, that is the region lying between the oil fields of the Maghreb and the Gulf of Guinea.

At the same time, US training for African forces was stepped up. Following the installation of the Bush administration in the United States, the African Crisis Response Initiative (ACRI) was converted in to the African Contingency Operations Training Assistance (ACOTA) which comes under the Pentagon's Africa Centre for Strategic Studies. ACOTA was given the role of offensive training as well as peace keeping and was linked to the training centres of the US Joint Combined Arms Training System (JCATS). The first JCATS centre in Africa was opened in Abuja, Nigeria in November 2003. By 2004 some 44 African countries were taking part in military training programmes covering offensive tactics and the transfer of military technology. According to US Col. Nestor Pino-Marina in charge of these programmes their objective is 'to bring integration into line with Pentagon norms and to install US equipment over the long term.'

In view of the location of the oil drillings all along the coast of the Gulf of Guinea and of the Red Sea pipeline at Port Sudan servicing the new Sudan oil field, there is talk of building a new pipeline linking the Chad-Cameroon pipeline, which debouches on the Gulf of Guinea, to the Sudan pipeline. As a background to these developments, it was noted in an earlier article by *Le Monde Diplomatique* (February 2003) that US and French naval units have been deployed in both East and West Africa. Task Force 150 is a naval unit operated jointly by the United States, Britain, France, Spain and Germany. A new US naval base is being established in São Tomé, where the most southerly oil drillings are being made in the Gulf of Guinea. In Djibouti on the Red Sea coast there was already a French naval base and to this has been added a permanent US base. *Le Monde Diplomatique,* in 2004, further reported some tensions arising there between the French and the United States. General Wald, the US European Command deputy commander, was said to spend a lot of time in Africa. In March 2004, he visited Morocco, Algeria, Nigeria, Angola, South Africa, Namibia, Gabon, São Tomé, Ghana, Niger and Tunisia, most of them oil states. After this tour, at a press conference in Washington for African journalists, he stressed that 'the United States and France had many interests in common' – one could say, oil for example, if their interests were compatible.

Mr Blair's Africa Commission

There is widespread concern about the African tragedies of violence and famine which have been greatly aggravated by the spread of HIV/AIDs throughout the continent. From the foregoing analysis of current international policies towards Africa, certain conclusions are obvious. The one-time colonial powers – including the United States – must acknowledge their responsibility for what has happened to Africa. The debts, which have now been repaid many times, should be cancelled; massive aid should be made available to rebuild the devastated infrastructure, improve education and health including measures to control the AIDS epidemic; arms sales and military training should cease; commodity prices should be controlled; corrupt practices should be prosecuted; dumping of subsidised products from the rich countries should be ended; and Africans should be encouraged in every way to develop their own capacities and methods of solving problems without tutelage.

Ethiopia: Students at risk of torture

Mass arrests and shootings of demonstrators in Addis Ababa in June left at least 26 dead and over 100 injured. According to Amnesty International, more than 1,500 students and other demonstrators who were detained were at risk of torture.

Amnesty condemned the excessive use of force by the police, who used live ammunition against mainly peaceful protestors – although some threw stones – and brutally beat them. 'The excessive and indiscriminate use of force is in contravention of international human rights standards,' said Kolawole Olaniyan, Amnesty International's Africa Programme Director. 'We call on the Ethiopian government to halt the police violence and set up an independent and impartial commission of inquiry into the killings that have already taken place, and to make those findings public.'

One female student, Shebray Delelegne, was killed when police reportedly opened fire on people attempting to block police vehicles carrying detained students. Six others were wounded in the incident. The death was called an 'accident' by officials who gave no further details.

Amnesty International also expressed serious concern for the fate of Chernet Tadesse, 31, a human rights defender and investigator for the Ethiopian Human Rights Council, who was arrested while collecting information on the arrests and deaths. The whereabouts after arrest yesterday of Andargachew Tsige, 48, are also unknown. He is a former deputy Mayor of Addis Ababa, a United Kingdom-based resident and author of a recent book criticising the government.

'We are very concerned for the safety of the detained students and others, who were, in most cases, peacefully demonstrating on their university campus or in the streets as a way of expressing their opinions,' said Kolawole Olaniyan. 'Many were beaten with batons and rifle butts and then taken away by the police.' Although police have said some have been released, most are believed to be still detained in police camps such as Sendafa police training college, 40 kms north of Addis Ababa.

The students were protesting about the provisional results of the parliamentary elections of 15 May. The protests defied the Prime Minister's one month post-election ban on demonstrations. The students were supporting opposition demands for an investigation into alleged voting irregularities, including reported arrests and beatings of opposition candidates. Provisional results of the parliamentary elections indicated a majority for Prime Minister Meles Zenawi's ruling Ethiopian People's Revolutionary Democratic Front coalition.

Tony Blair convened his Commission for Africa in Addis last October. Prime Minister Meles Zenawi joined in the deliberations.

Mr Blair's Africa Commission has sought to meet some of these demands. The Commissioners include Africans who will have the task of implementing their conclusions – the President of Tanzania, the Prime Minister of Ethiopia, the General Secretary of the Economic Commission for Africa, a UN Under Secretary and Executive Director of UN Habitat sitting with Sir Bob Geldorf, Tony Blair and Gordon Brown and the former head of the International Monetary Fund, M. Camdessus. Optimists have noted some good signs: for once the responsibility of the corruptors has been recognised along with that of the corrupted, the commitment to end the debt burden and make large sums available in international aid, the emphasis on public education and health with detailed costings over the years, the need to make trade fairer without subsidised competition from the rich countries.

The Commission's proposals are being put to the leaders of the 'Great Powers' and of the European Union. What will matter is not the words that are agreed but the action that follows. The pessimists expect little to change. Laurence Cockcroft, chair of Transparency International, has pointed out (*The Guardian* 10.03.05) that many cases of corruption have been clearly established over the years, but no one has yet been prosecuted. The World Development Movement argued (29.04.04) at the announcement of the Commission's establishment that there was no need for more research, all the problems were well known, but 'what was lacking was the political will in the industrialised world to make good on existing commitments and make use of the wealth of knowledge and the strength of feeling in Africa in favour of lasting and radical change'. The director of The African Foundation for Development (AFFORD), an organisation of the African diaspora, has put it even more strongly: 'Most of us in any case are suffering from acute "consultitis" – we're all researched out.' The British aid community, represented by British Overseas NGOs for Development (BOND) which links nearly 300 organisations working in the development sector, has welcomed the Commission, but many Africans complain of the proliferation of non-governmental organisations in each territory with competing and often conflicting interests that take up an inordinate amount of time for their African counterparts to deal with.

If the Commission's proposals are to be realised there are some big changes that will have to be made in British and European Government practice, before discussion even begins with the United States over its agricultural subsidies and protectionist measures. The new European reform of the European Common Agricultural Policy involves payments to farmers in place of subsidies. This reform, according to experts (Paul Goodison and Colin Stoneman, *Review of African Political Economy*, no. 102, 2004) has the result of a) increasing European output, b) making the European market less attractive for developing country producers of temperate agricultural exports and c) enhancing the price competitiveness of European Union exports. A more direct change in British practice will mean, further, the ending of aid with water supplies being made conditional on privatisation and on the employment of large non-African water companies. It will be recalled that one member of the Commission, M. Camdessus, when he was Director General of the International Monetary Fund, pressed everywhere for measures of privatisation to be part of the structural reforms which were made a necessary condition for the receipt of aid.

Governments that are praised for their successes are generally those such as Uganda and Mozambique, which have gone furthest in carrying out International Monetary Fund policies. These have had the result of increased growth but at the same time widening inequalities of income and wealth. Other countries commended for economic growth are some of the oil states. There is no mention in the Commission's report of the key question of military aid and of the foreign support for governments of oil states, where the human rights abuses of dictatorial rule are endemic. Commission member Anna Tibaijuka has stressed the importance of the title given to the Commission's report 'Our Common Interest', which harks back to the title of the Brandt Commission report in 1983, *Common Crisis: North–South Cooperation for World Recovery*. Aid is not so much humanitarian as self-protection.

Many Africans say that these are just more promises after twenty years, during which the state of Africa has worsened! To offset such criticism, the new report emphasises that there are important new things happening in Africa that can be built on. The first is that the African Union, which replaces the old Organisation of African States, is prepared for the first time to intervene as a peer group in the

Tanzania's privatised water deal cancelled

The Tanzanian Government has cancelled its deal with Biwater, the French-owned but British–based water company. In 2003, Biwater contracted to bring clean water to the capital, Dar es Salaam, and the surrounding region within five years by installing new pipes. The $140m (£76.5m) World Bank-funded privatisation scheme was supported by the United Kingdom government. It was one of the most ambitious in Africa and was intended to be a model for how the world's poorest communities could be lifted out of poverty.

The Tanzanian Government claims that no new domestic pipework has been installed under the contract, the company has not spent the money it had promised, water quality has declined, and that revenue has decreased. 'The company has failed to produce the goods,' Tanzania's water minister, Edward Lowassa, said.

A spokesman for the water company denied the accusations and said a case had been filed against the Tanzanian government for alleged breach of contract. He accepted that the project was well behind schedule and that no pipes had been installed, but he claimed water quality and quantity had improved and that 10,000 new customers had been signed up.

problems of the member states. Its first test is the Sudan. The second new happening is said to be the formation of NEPAD – New Economic Partnership for African Development. This is not particularly new. The occasion of the Blair Commission report to be presented to the G8 in July 2005 is little more than a rerun of the NEPAD presentation at the 2002 G8 meeting in Alberta, Canada, to which Presidents Thabo Mbeki, Olusegun Obasanjo, Abdoulaye Wade and Abdel Aziz Bouteflika were invited. On that occasion the Nigerian President pointedly told the G8 leaders that 'how they dealt with the debt issue would be a good yardstick for our expectations as to how much you are prepared to keep your side of the bargain in our new partnership.'

What hopes were aroused then among Africans? Discussing the outcome of this G8 meeting, the African journalist, Yao Graham, editor of the Ghanaian journal *African Agenda*, quoted (in the issue of Vol.5, nos. 2&3, 2002) the report of a 'Continental Experts' meeting on NEPAD and the African Union, hosted by the Africa Institute of South Africa, a think-tank closely identified with the South African political establishment. The 300 participants concluded, according to Yao Graham, that

'the Nepad initiative was located within the Washington consensus and as a result was likely to perpetuate and reinforce the subjugation of Africa in the global system, the enclavity of African economies and the marginalisation of Africa's people.'

The privatisation scheme was facilitated by British aid money. The Department for International Development paid Adam Smith International, sister organisation of the free market think-tank Adam Smith Institute, more than £500,000 to provide advice to the Tanzanian government. More than £250,000 of that sum was spent by Adam Smith International on a video which included the words: 'Our old industries are dry like crops and privatisation brings the rain.'

According to Dave Timms of the World Development Movement, Tanzania was forced to privatise its water as a condition of international debt forgiveness. 'The International Monetary Fund forced water privatisation on one of the poorest countries in the world in order to benefit western water companies,' he said.

The collapse of the contract throws into question other water privatisations planned around the world, and the British government's involvement in them. Resentment against private water monopolies is growing, and there have been demonstrations in South America, Africa, the Caribbean, and Asia. Many western companies are accused of profiting from the poor and raising prices above what they can afford.

The Department for International Development has paid more than £36m in the past seven years to Adam Smith International and PricewaterhouseCoopers to advise countries on privatising utilities.

It is just this question of partnership that is at issue. Blair has sold the case for helping Africa very much as a common interest – of the North and the South – the North fearing the dangers of violence spreading from the South. But a partnership must be on the basis of equality between the partners – and that simply does not exist, except between them as human beings. To build a true partnership, the North would have to accept responsibility for the past, but there have been no expressions of responsibility from the Colonial Powers. Gordon Brown, in January 2005, said that Britain had nothing to apologise for from its colonial past. Thanks to the successful publicising of a book on *Empire* by Niall Ferguson, the British Empire is being seen as a great philanthropic enterprise of modernisation, which the Americans are being asked to emulate. The tragic condition of Africa is said by Ferguson to be the result of prematurely ending that process. This is a bit rich coming from a Scotsman who holds a chair at Harvard, in the very place where colonial rule was ended, leading to successful development. The fundamental problem for Africa, as Anna Tibaijka recognises, is the need to encourage African self-confidence.

Michaela Wrong has quoted a Kenyan business journalist saying, 'The phenomenon of capital flight is essentially born out of an inferiority complex' (*New Statesman*, 14.03.05). The offers of aid to Africa are still being made, as previously by the International Monetary Fund, with conditionalities attached – of ending corruption and establishing good governance, as if these were entirely African responsibilities. If Mr. Blair's Africa Commission were to be seen by Africans as a truly generous act of human solidarity, the language of paternalism would have to be changed and the practice of exploitation ended. Without such a major shift in approach and action the whole exercise will remain, in an election year, the most sophisticated piece of spin doctoring that even Mr Blair has so far elaborated.

Take the arms companies out of government

Every year, around £900 million of public money is spent subsidising the sale of UK weaponry around the world.

Why? Because arms companies wield immense political power and influence within government.

It's time to stop arms companies calling the shots.

For a free Call the Shots campaign pack, please call 020 7281 0297 or email enquiries@caat.org.uk

www.caat.org.uk

CAMPAIGN AGAINST ARMS TRADE

Ron Todd
1927 – 2005

Ron Todd died on 30 April 2005. Here he is remembered by Ken Coates and Bruce Kent. Ron's early days are also recalled in his own words.

Ron Todd died of leukaemia at the age of 78 after suffering the condition with characteristic bravery. Ron had led Britain's largest trade union through its most difficult transition, in the full efflorescence of Thatcherism. He was elected General Secretary of the Transport and General Workers' Union in 1984, when his predecessor, Moss Evans, retired early. The succession was hotly contested, and his opponent, George Wright, the Secretary of the Welsh Region of the Union, gathered strong support. Ron won the election with a majority of nearly forty-five thousand. Just over forty per cent of the Union's one and a half million members voted, and some of George Wright's backers challenged the result. Moss Evans insisted that the election was a valid one, but Ron Todd was unwilling to accept the leadership on the basis of a contested vote, and it was his influence that brought about the rerun of the ballot. He won handsomely, in June 1985, with a majority of nearly seventy-seven thousand. There were no further challenges, and he remained the undisputed leader for seven years.

Ron Todd's integrity was clear and crystalline. His members needed him, at a time when they were under fire from the Government. In one industry after another, Mrs. Thatcher sought to wear down the Unions.

The most obvious set-piece battle of those days was of course, the miners' strike. Ron did what he could to bring support to the miners' cause: but this was not easy. I remember conducting a class for Rolls Royce shop stewards at the beginning of the strike, at a time when the whole Labour movement was energetically engaged in the miners' cause. The stewards described how they passed a bucket round the workshop to collect donations for the strikers. Everyone chipped in, often with folding money. But later, after the battles between pickets and working miners in North Nottinghamshire, and the intense propaganda in the press about the miners' lack of a national ballot, this spontaneous support began to ebb.

Large amounts of money were still collected, but this had to be done discreetly, by personally approaching the members in the workplace, since any public identification with the strike would provoke hostility, and might prevent some of the members from contributing. The Transport and General Workers' Union was not immune from these kinds of pressure, as Ron Todd discovered when he sought to foster action in solidarity. It failed.

The miners went down to defeat, and Mrs. Thatcher continued her offensive. By 1989 she was ready to take on the dockers, by annulling the Dock Labour Scheme, which had been established by Ernest Bevin during the Second World War. This had given dock workers a real measure of workers' control over hiring and firing, so that it was an obvious target in Thatcher's Holy War for management prerogatives. Ron Todd did what he could, but the weather was adverse for militant trade unionism, and the Dock Labour Scheme, too, went down.

These defeats were all reflected in the Labour Party as a vigorous struggle erupted between the Union and the Party leadership of Neil Kinnock.

These were the dying years of the Cold War, and in Britain they were the years of unilateral nuclear disarmament. Ron Todd had taken up the banner of unilateral nuclear disarmament from Frank Cousins, who had opposed Hugh Gaitskell's efforts to reverse the Labour Party's decision to oppose Britain's nuclear weapons programmes. Ron was very much a patriot, a former Marine who had been on board the *Amethyst* during its last voyage down the Yangtze through the encircling actions of the Chinese Red Army. But the finality of nuclear weapons persuaded Ron, like many other ex-servicemen, that annihilation was not an acceptable mode of warfare. He wanted to ban the bomb.

Having taken up the anti-nuclear cause, Ron's first political engagement during his leadership period was at the European Nuclear Disarmament Convention in Perugia, in July 1984, to which he led a strong delegation from his Union's General Executive Council. This included leaders of the busmen, the dockers in London and Hull, and the Union's President.

The END Convention brought together an important part of the European political establishment, including two European Commissioners and a number of notable political spokesmen. But it also brought together some hundreds of rank and file activists, who taken together were a somewhat turbulent bunch. Ron had every opportunity to demonstrate his famous tolerance when being heckled by some of these young people, who had no respect for age, experience or seniority. However, in those early days he could call on the strong support of Neil Kinnock as a famous unilateralist. But soon it became evident that this situation was going to change.

After the 1987 General Election defeat, Neil Kinnock decided that unilateral disarmament was a millstone, and that it must become a major preoccupation of his leadership to get rid of it. A bitter battle broke out behind the scenes in the Labour Party, coupled with an infinitely subtle war of manoeuvre and positioning. All too many of the young rebels who had catcalled Ron Todd in Perugia, accusing him of 'bureaucracy', were gradually to find the need to defend the deterrent. One of the young Turks at Perugia was Denis MacShane, until recently a front bench pillar of the Blair Labour Government, than which no political formation is today more innocent of pacifism in any form.

Ron Todd fought that good fight, for his Union members, for those trapped in declining industries, for his political comrades and for the peace movement. He will be remembered with love when those who connived to outsmart him and put him down are only remembered, if at all, with contempt.

Ken Coates

* * *

No one gave a better link with the Trade Union movement

The picture of Ron Todd on the front of the printed order of service on 10 May 2005 was a wonderful choice. It was Ron just as we all knew him. Direct, confident, open, a gentle smile, well-tanned and, of course, wearing his Transport and General Workers' tie. May 10 was much more a celebration than a service; certainly a marvellous gathering of those who loved and admired him. There were of course members of his family who all meant so much to him. They were the centre of his life, as all the pictures and mementoes in his small house in Surrey Road made clear.

As well as family, there were old comrades from the Marines with banners and medals, plenty of trade union stalwarts headed by Rodney Bickerstaffe and Tony Woodley, lots of local friends from Dagenham, and a strong contingent from CND with our striking new yellow banner. Tony Benn and John Cryer represented different generations of the Labour Party – the old rather than the new. The Dagenham Football Social Club hall was packed out to the car park.

No wonder. Everyone had their own good memories of Ron, a rock of consistency and common sense in a world where opportunism rather than principle rules. His description of the new Kinnock/Blair activists as 'sharp-suited socialists with cordless telephones' came straight out of his own East End working class roots. Socialism was a word of which he was proud. It was the religion of his life.

Proudly an ex-service Marine, he never gave up his conviction that nuclear weapons, illegal and immoral, give this country less, not more, security. A hands-on campaigner he certainly was in his time. Hopping out of the T & G limousine he joined the last stage of the 1986 walk from Faslane to Burghfield and stuck it out over many miles despite a large collection of bloody blisters.

His poem 'Walks with my Wife' was printed on that service sheet. It was a great tribute to his dear friend and partner of so many years, his wife Josephine, who died before him. They met when 16 and married at 18. 'So many happy memories...' begins one line of that poem.

No one gave a better link with the Trade Union movement than did our Vice President and friend, Ron Todd. We will all greatly miss him.

Bruce Kent, CND

* * *

The story of Ron's early days ... in his own words

Working with a snake for a quack doctor, being punished for setting a priest's cassock alight, and having a rivet pierce his finger in an industrial accident ... all were recalled in Ron Todd's memoirs which he started just before his death.

He was born on 11th March 1927 at 4 Apsley Road, Walthamstow, East London, next to the market where his father worked as a street trader.

'The stall next to my father's was held by a quack doctor named Laurie Jameson, who sold herbs and powders for every conceivable ailment,' wrote Ron. 'The main attraction of this stall for me was his pet boa constrictor which hung from the slats. Laurie would coil the snake round my neck, and when a small crowd gathered he would start his spiel. He used to tell me that the snake and I got on well together and he intended to ask my father if I would be allowed to tour the country with him. I saw myself becoming famous, but my father told me not to take any of Laurie's stories or promises seriously.'

Ron went to school from the age of five at St Patrick's Roman Catholic school. As an altar boy he was carrying the staff with a candle as the priest conducted the 'Stations of the Cross.' A friend asked him if he was going to the mobile roller skating rink which was visiting the area. 'As my attention was distracted, my candle ignited the priest's cassock, and what I can only describe as pandemonium broke out ... I was dragged by Sister Mary de Lourde into the vestry where I was unceremoniously unfrocked. I was told I would burn in the fires of hell, which seemed an excessive punishment compared to a priest losing one arm of his cassock. I was then told to kneel and do a penance of ten Hail Marys, which I did punctuated by slaps on the back of my head. Hail Mary full of grace (SLAP), blessed art thou among women (SLAP), and so on.'

In 1941 he got a job making army boots with a riveting machine. A friend shouted out to him, which once more distracted his attention, and he felt a blow to his hand.

'When I looked down, the index finger of my right hand was going white, and as I turned my hand to examine any damage I saw the head of a rivet counter sink in the middle of my nail, and on the other side of my finger the rivet was bent over. We finished up with Mr Putnam [the boss] himself driving me to hospital where the rivet was removed – and then given to me by the doctor as a souvenir.' On the return journey to the factory the boss gave him a lecture on paying attention to what he was doing. Ron eventually lost the rivet, but always remembered the advice.

Sadly, that was as far as Ron got with his written reminiscences.

THE BERTRAND RUSSELL PEACE FOUNDATION
DOSSIER

2005   Number 16

IRAQ: CUTS IN THE OCCUPATION FORCES?

An 'Options' paper on reducing British military personnel in Iraq, by the British Defence Minister John Reid, was leaked to The Mail on Sunday newspaper and published on 10 July 2005. We have reproduced all that was published there – part 5, 'Technical details', was not published in the newspaper. In the interests of clarity, some factual explanations have been added in square [] brackets.

Options for future UK force posture in Iraq
Paper by Secretary of State SECRET - UK EYES ONLY

1. ISSUE
We will need to reach decisions later this year on likely future UK force structure and disposition in Iraq into 2006.

This paper sets out some of the key contextual considerations; identifies areas of uncertainty; sets out what we know of US planning and possible expectations on the UK contribution; and assesses the potential impact on UK decision making.

2. Decisions on coalition, and within that, UK force levels will be governed by four factors, all of which are subject to a greater or lesser degree of uncertainty:
● Internal Iraqi pressure for further force posture changes.
● Successful progress in the potential process and extension/renewal of United Nations Security Council Resolution 1546. [UN resolution authorising allied troops presence in Iraq]
● The continued development of the capability of the Iraqi Security Forces (ISF).
● The security situation.

3. None of this, however, undermines the Multinational Force Iraq (MNF-I) [The Multinational Force of Allied troops in Iraq] broad security strategy of:
a) Working with the Iraqis to contain and restrain the insurgency.
b) Assisting and encouraging the development of Iraqi security forces and structures which can progressively assume responsibility for all aspects of security including dealing with the insurgency, and thereby:
c) Enable MNF-I force reductions and eventual withdrawal.

4. US POSITION

US political military thinking is still evolving. But there is a strong US military desire for significant force reductions to bring relief to overall US commitment levels.

Emerging US plans assume that 14 out of 18 provinces could be handed over to Iraqi control by early 2006, allowing a reduction in overall MNF-I from 176,000 down to 66,000.

There is, however, a debate between the Pentagon/Centcom [US military Central Command] who favour a relatively bold reduction in force numbers, and MNF-I whose approach is more cautious.

The next MNF-I review of campaign progress due in late June may help clarify thinking and provide an agreed framework for the way ahead.

5. (Technical details – not published)

6. UK POLICY CONSIDERATIONS

The current ministerially endorsed policy position is that the UK should not:
a) Agree to any changes to the UK area of responsibility.
b) Agree to any specific deployments outside Multinational Division South East. [Not get involved in operations outside area around Basra under UK control]
c) Agree to any specific increases in the roughly 8,500 UK service personnel currently deployed in Iraq.

7. Looking further ahead, we have a clear UK military aspiration to hand over to Iraqi control in Al Muthanna and Maysan provinces [two of the four provinces around Basra in UK control] in October 2005 and in the other two Multinational Division South East provinces, Dhi Qar and Basra [the other two UK run provinces] in April 2006.

This in turn should lead to a reduction in the total level of UK commitment in Iraq to around 3,000 personnel, i.e. small scale, by mid 2006.

This should lead to an estimated halving in the costs which fall to the reserve [the UK Treasury Reserve], around £1 billion per annum currently. Though it is not clear exactly when this reduction might manifest itself, it would not be before around the end of 2006.

8. None of this however, represents a ministerially endorsed plan. There is a good deal more military analysis to do which is under way. We will need to consider handling of other Multinational Division South East allies.

The Japanese reconstruction battalion [Japan has 550 engineers in UK area of Iraq] will for example be reluctant to stay in Al Muthanna if force protection is solely provided by the Iraqis. [The Australian position, which is highly influenced by the Japanese presence, may also be uncertain.]

NOTE

I will bring further and more specific proposals to DOP-I [The Defence and

Overseas Policy, Iraq sub committee of the Cabinet chaired by the Prime Minister] for the future UK force posture in Iraq, including handover to Iraqi control and subsequent UK military drawdown.

John Reid

IS BRITAIN'S NUCLEAR ARSENAL TO BE REPLACED?

Britain's nuclear arsenal comprises four nuclear-armed submarines, each carrying up to 16 Trident missiles, with three nuclear warheads on each missile. Each warhead has an explosive power of up to 100 kilotons. This is eight times the force of the atomic bomb that was dropped on Hiroshima, killing an estimated 140,000 people.

Is it true, as *The Independent* alleges, that a decision to replace Trident with a new generation of nuclear weapons has now been taken, but not publicly announced? The estimated cost is said to exceed £10 billion.

On 2 May 2005, shortly before the General Election, *The Independent* reported a senior defence source who said 'The decision [to replace Trident] has been taken in principle very recently. US law does not allow the US to build bombs for us. We have to build our own.' Although Trident is not due to be decommissioned until 2024, 'there is a very long lead time,' the source added. 'That is why the decision in principle had to be taken now.'

Aldermaston, where Britain's nuclear warheads are built, has been hiring physicists and mathematicians for the past year.

These developments take place whilst the British Government urges Iran and other countries not to develop nuclear weapons. At the same time, the Nuclear Non-Proliferation Treaty has suffered a serious reversal at its recent review conference in New York, after prolonged stonewalling by the United States. No effective way forward was found to halting the development of new nuclear weapons by the nuclear powers, nor in halting the spread of nuclear weapons to some countries who do not have them.

Of course, Britain's current nuclear arsenal comes with a very large operational price tag. This eats in to the military budget. The National Audit Office recently highlighted the intense pressure on supplies and personnel in the British Armed Forces, and the reliance on urgent procurements to fill gaps in equipment levels. Personal accounts from servicemen and women in Iraq indicate that these gaps still go unfilled, sometimes with fatal consequences. Interestingly, the Audit Office notes that shortfalls in Nuclear, Biological and Chemical consumables 'could not be rectified in time' for Operation TELIC, the invasion of Iraq.

Senior military personnel are well aware of the high cost of maintaining a nuclear arsenal, and developing a new one. Other programmes they see as vital, such as the construction of new aircraft carriers, are scaled back to pay for nuclear weapons.

QUESTIONS FOR PRESIDENT BUSH

More than 560,000 Americans have already signed the letter to President Bush initiated by Congressman John Conyers, Jr. It asks probing questions about the Downing Street Memo of 23 July 2002, which recorded United States and United Kingdom early planning for the war on Iraq (see Spokesman 86). The Memo and all the other leaked documents about British preparations for the war have been brought together in The Dodgiest Dossier *(Spokesman Books £4).*

Honourable George W. Bush
President of the United States of America
1600 Pennsylvania Ave, N.W.
Washington, D.C. 20005

Dear Mr. President:
We the undersigned write because of our concern regarding recent disclosures of a Downing Street Memo in the London *Times*, comprising the minutes of a meeting of Prime Minister Tony Blair and his top advisers. These minutes indicate that the United States and Great Britain agreed, by the summer of 2002, to attack Iraq, well before the invasion and before you even sought Congressional authority to engage in military action, and that US officials were deliberately manipulating intelligence to justify the war.

Among other things, the British government document quotes a high-ranking British official as stating that by July 2002, Bush had made up his mind to take military action. Yet, a month later, you stated you were still willing to 'look at all options' and that there was 'no timetable' for war. Secretary of Defence, Donald Rumsfeld, flatly stated that '[t]he president has made no such determination that we should go to war with Iraq.'

In addition, the origins of the false contention that Iraq had weapons of mass destruction remain a serious and lingering question about the lead up to the war. There is an ongoing debate about whether this was the result of a 'massive intelligence failure,' in other words a mistake, or the result of intentional and deliberate manipulation of intelligence to justify the case for war. The memo appears to resolve that debate as well, quoting the head of British intelligence as indicating that in the United States 'the intelligence and facts were being fixed around the policy.'

As a result of these concerns, we would ask that you respond to the following questions:

1) Do you or anyone in your administration dispute the accuracy of the leaked document?

2) Were arrangements being made, including the recruitment of allies, before you sought Congressional authorisation to go to war? Did you or anyone in your Administration obtain Britain's commitment to invade prior to this time?

3) Was there an effort to create an ultimatum about weapons inspectors in order to

help with the justification for the war as the minutes indicate?
4) At what point in time did you and Prime Minister Blair first agree it was necessary to invade Iraq?
5) Was there a coordinated effort with the US intelligence community and/or British officials to 'fix' the intelligence and facts around the policy as the leaked document states?

These are the same questions 89 Members of Congress, led by Rep. John Conyers, Jr., submitted to you on May 5, 2005. As citizens and taxpayers, we believe it is imperative that our people be able to trust our government and our commander in chief when you make representations and statements regarding our nation engaging in war. As a result, we would ask that you publicly respond to these questions as promptly as possible.

Thank you for your prompt attention to this matter.

US RESTARTS PLUTONIUM 238 PRODUCTION

The United States is preparing to produce highly radioactive plutonium 238 for the first time since the end of the Cold War. Officials say that the plutonium is being produced for 'national security'.

The isotope, many hundred times more radioactive than plutonium 239, which is used in nuclear weapons, is to be produced at the Idaho National Laboratory close to the Yellowstone National Park in Wyoming. Officials involved in the $1.5bn (£800m) programme, which is intended to produce around 300lb of the material in the next 30 years, say the bulk of the plutonium will be used in secret projects but refuse to provide further details. The material has previously been used in batteries to power deep space probes such as Cassini as well as underwater surveillance and espionage equipment.

'The real reason we're starting production is for national security,' Timothy Frazier, head of radio-isotope power systems at the Energy Department, told *The New York Times* (June 2005). The United States has not made plutonium 238 since the 1980s when production was based at the Savannah River plant in South Carolina with some other work done in New Mexico and Tennessee. Since then it has relied on ageing stockpiles of the material or else on imports from Russia. The new programme will concentrate production at the Idaho facility in an effort to minimise the risk of leakage or contamination involving the 50,000 drums of hazardous and radioactive waste it is expected to make.

Local groups fear the programme will present considerable public health risks. Mary Woollen-Mitchell of Keep Yellowstone Nuclear Free said: 'They are concentrating all this production in just one place but it has never really been done safely anywhere. We're sceptical when they say, 'We know enough to make sure it's safe and to avoid an accident'. When they have spoken to us they say the majority of it will be for secret missions but they don't talk about the remainder.

I worry about whether it will be involved in the weaponisation of space.'

In his interview, Mr Frazier adamantly denied that the plutonium would be involved in military projects in space, though it has previously been used to power vessels that have travelled to those parts of space where there is insufficient sunlight to power solar panels. One unidentified federal scientist who helps the military plan space missions told the newspaper that the plutonium might be used in future projects to power compact spy satellites that would be difficult to detect. 'It's going to be a tough world in the next one or two decades and this may be needed,' he said. 'Technologically, it makes sense.'

Sources: www.space4peace.org, The Independent 28 June 2005

'OUTSOURCING' TORTURE – AMNESTY

We have paid close attention to United States involvement in torture and abuse of detainees, ever since the first reports in late 2002 about 'rendition' of captives to other countries for interrogation (see Spokesman 81, 82, and 83). Amnesty International's recent report on human rights abuses by the United States, Guantánamo and beyond: The continuing pursuit of unchecked executive power, *contains a wealth of detail on these activities. We reprint some excerpts.*

'…The report points to an overarching war mentality adopted by the US administration since 11 September 2001 which has led it to manipulate or jettison basic human rights protections for detainees, including instances of the USA refusing to recognise that United Nations human rights experts have the mandate to raise concerns about US actions in the "war on terror". For example, UN Special Rapporteurs have raised allegations of extrajudicial executions by US forces, only to have the US reject such concerns out of hand. In April 2005, the mandate of the UN Independent Expert on the Situation of Human Rights in Afghanistan was not renewed. This is alleged to have been the result of US government pressure. The former postholder has said that he believes the non-renewal of his mandate was due to the USA's dislike of his insistence that he should be allowed to visit detainees in US custody in Afghanistan, particularly in light of allegations of torture and ill-treatment of such detainees.

Over a year after the Abu Ghraib torture scandal broke, and as evidence of torture and other cruel, inhuman or degrading treatment by US forces in the "war on terror" continues to mount, not one US agent has been charged with "war crimes" or "torture" under US law. In over 70 per cent of announced official actions taken in response to substantiated allegations of abuse, the punishment has been non-judicial or administrative. While a small number of mainly low-ranking soldiers have been subjected to courts-martial, members of the administration, who from the outset have claimed that the USA treats all detainees humanely and that any abuses have been the actions of a few aberrant soldiers, have remained free of independent investigation despite possible criminal responsibility in abuses. Congress has failed to initiate an independent commission of inquiry, as Amnesty International has sought. The current Attorney General, like his predecessor possibly involved in a conspiracy to immunise US agents from criminal liability for torture and war crimes under US law, has not appointed a special prosecutor to pursue this matter as Amnesty International and others have urged.

As the culture of impunity and military leniency grows, including in cases in which Afghan and Iraqi detainees have died as a result of abuses by US agents, the administration continues to seek to try members of the "enemy" for war crimes in front of military commissions – executive bodies, not independent or impartial courts. It has appealed against a federal court ruling that the military commission procedures are unlawful because the defendant can be excluded from proceedings. Amnesty International reiterates its total opposition to the military commissions, which violate international fair trial standards in numerous ways ...

… Thousands of detainees remain in US custody in Iraq – a country which President Bush repeated on 12 April 2005 has become "a central front in the war on terror" since the US-led invasion in March 2003. Hundreds remain in US custody in Afghanistan, with some in Bagram air base having been detained without trial and virtually incommunicado for more than a year. The International Committee of the Red Cross (ICRC), the only international organisation with access to some of the detainees in Afghanistan, reiterated on 29 March 2005 that it was "increasingly concerned by the fact that the US authorities have not resolved the question of their legal status and of the applicable legal framework". In addition, the USA is holding an unknown number of detainees in secret incommunicado custody in unknown locations and unknown conditions in cases that may amount to "disappearance". Evidence that the US authorities have "outsourced" torture via secret detainee transfers to other countries continues to come to light ...'

The full text is available online at:
http://web.amnesty.org/library/Index/ENGAMR510632005

CAMBRIDGE

... at the cutting edge

The Ethics and Politics of Asylum
Liberal Democracy and the Response to Refugees
Matthew J. Gibney
'This is the only book length study available of the ethics of asylum ... It is intelligent, perceptive, and lucidly written. Anyone interested in questions about refugees should read this book.'
Joseph H. Carens, University of Toronto
£40.00 | HB | 0 521 80417 5 | 298pp
£15.99 | PB | 0 521 00937 5

Deadly Connections
States that Sponsor Terrorism
Daniel Byman

'... there is no other current book on the same topic. I learned a tremendous amount by reading it.'
Karin von Hippel, London School of Economics
'Dan Byman has written what will likely become the standard text on state-sponsored terrorism.'
Bruce Hoffman, author of Inside Terrorism and former Director of RAND Corporation, Washington DC
Publication June 2005
c.**£15.00** | HB | 0 521 83973 4 | 280pp

forthcoming

forthcoming

The Market for Force
The Consequences of Privatizing Security
Deborah D. Avant
The first serious attempt to grapple with the difficult trade-offs involved in controlling private security in the global market.
Publication June 2005
c.**£40.00** | HB | 0 521 85026 6 | 320pp
c.**£16.99** | PB | 0 521 61535 6

www.cambridge.org   **CAMBRIDGE UNIVERSITY PRESS**

Reviews

Labour's last leader

Mark Stuart, *John Smith: A Life*, Politico's Publishing, 509 pages, hardback ISBN 1842751263, £25

Mark Stuart has set out to recover, for John Smith, 'his own wee corner in Labour's recent history, nothing more, nothing less'. More generally his book seeks to 'reconnect New Labour with its past'. He has approached his first task with diligence and sympathy, but is less impressive in his attempts to address the second.

The problem is that, in a very real sense, Smith was the last Leader of the Labour Party, and that New Labour was in fact new precisely in as much as it had no past, or rather that it derived its novelty from repudiating its past.

Stuart establishes beyond reasonable doubt that Smith was a decent man, strongly motivated by impeccable old Labour values. His successor held these values in profound contempt, and saw them as a permanent reproach to his idea of modernity. But, for him, modernity was the systematic unleashing of the market, red in tooth and claw, to savage every vestige of public and private life. Tony Blair thought the unthinkable, and promoted its Gospel. It is not a little bit surprising that Smith was deemed inconvenient within the Blairite memory, and that it has taken it ten years to summon up the courage to mention him, albeit briefly, without obvious contempt.

Smith rose to political influence in the age of the mixed economy, and was strongly influenced by Hugh Gaitskell. Gaitskell's testament can be found in the elaborate Charter of Principles which he appended to the Labour Party's Clause IV, after a loud, and not very persuasive contest to revise that article of the Labour Party's constitution. Gaitskell did not seek to annul Labour's commitment to public ownership. But he did seek to hedge it about with other desiderata.

By the time, thirty years on, that Jack Straw came to see John Smith, recently installed as Labour Leader, in order to argue for the rescinding (recasting) of the Clause, Labour had been out of office for a demoralisingly long period. John Smith did not believe that the repudiation of historic doctrines would make much difference to his electoral prospects. He was confident that his turn would come. But Jack Straw did not believe this. Somewhat emblematically, his attempts to persuade his own local Labour Party were a failure. They consented to his publishing a pamphlet containing his views, but only with the disclaimer: 'This pamphlet contains Jack's personal views. They have not been endorsed by the Blackburn Constituency Labour Party'.

Straw's meeting with Smith 'began in a frosty atmosphere, and went from bad to worse'.

Smith was not a partisan of the old Clause IV by any means. Indeed, it can be argued that he never understood the central thrust which endeared it to generations of Labour voters. This did not involve a commitment to nationalisation of absolutely everything, but did involve the only recognition by a major political Party, or any major social institution, of the yearning for freedom among working people: and for democracy as the best practicable approach to that freedom. Such democracy, they believed, should not stop at the factory gate. Labour people were not objecting to the unseemly rules which flowed from authoritarian ownership, although these were obscene, and have, under the rule of Mrs. Thatcher and Mr. Blair, become more so, as the rich lists have got richer, and economic power has ever more resolutely concentrated itself in fewer and fewer hands. Indeed, the fundamental objection to this unjust order of things has always been the subordination of one man or woman to another. 'No man', said William Morris, 'is good enough to be another's master.' So far, no woman has been either.

Stuart argues that Clause IV was 'never implemented' by Labour in Government. But the search for 'the best obtainable system of popular administration and control of each industry or service' can fairly be said to have haunted the Wilson administrations, especially between 1974 and 1979.

Wilson had set up the Bullock Enquiry in order to exorcise this spectre. But for a long time, Labour people of the right as well as the left, showed their strong concern to reopen the issue of democracy in industry. I think I can claim to be innocent of any taint of Gaitskellism, but I do recall the approaches that I received from a variety of former Gaitskellites who were most anxious to hasten the process which they correctly perceived as being delayed by the researches of Lord Bullock.

All these matters are forgotten today, but in the seventies they were dominant. The truth is that the trade unions had established a much more powerful position in society than had the Labour Party. This teetered in and out of government, not really knowing what to do, whilst trade union defensive power continuously and steadily augmented. Unless this power could find a positive expression, it would be predominantly negative, controlling or ameliorating those matters to which it had the greatest objection, without, at any point, initiating positive alternatives. It had always, in Labour's long schizophrenia, fallen to the political wing to propose new positive measures. But parliamentary socialism had pretty well dried up.

The defeat of the Bullock Report was only the culmination of an official battle, a war of manoeuvre within committees. But the defeat of the idea that working people could play a decisive part in the framing of overall social goals and objectives was the beginning of the present murrain. It led directly to the reign of Thatcher, who systematically sought to roll back the defensive powers of trade unions, and diminished, in one area after another, their residual influence.

It was not Smith's fault that he inherited this moral wilderness. It was to give rise directly to nullities like Blair. Old Labour had defended a mixed economy, without feeling any need to trumpet its virtues. But the revision of Clause IV, itself by the 1990s an archaic document, was not about defining the scope of a mix. It was about annulling that mix. This has not proved to be a popular task, and it has required the intense Thatcherite zeal of Mr. Blair to hold his reluctant Party together whilst the annulment has gathered momentum. The motor of this process has been patronage, liberally applied to smother any vestige of democracy. But that is why New Labour cannot recover its history without regenerating antibodies which would quickly destroy it.

John Smith emerges from this rather good book as a victim of the tumultuous pressures which pulled here and there, as the Labour Party sought to contend with the world of neo-liberalism. I encountered him very late, when Robin Cook brought him out to the European Parliament, during his preparation for the leadership elections which he won. I was the first person he saw, because I had been campaigning, with Stuart Holland, for full employment, and the adoption of the Delors programme of Keynes-plus employment creation, and he met with Henry McCubbin, Peter Crampton and myself in my office to talk about the campaign which we had been running. This ultimately established the European Parliament's Temporary Committee on Employment, which was the last serious attempt to rally support for the Delors programme. We lost this battle, and now unemployment is corroding the very basis of European unity. Blair, far from offering an alternative, is a serious part of the problem.

If John Smith were to return among us, what I learnt of his behaviour during the short time that we were working in harness, leads me to think that he might well have become one of the more lethal critics of the present establishment which calls itself Labour. He will not rejoin us, but he has never left us. Will his legacy come to fruition in the post-New Labour epoch? Or must we anticipate an even steeper decline into authoritarianism and nihilism than is already being accomplished by those in power over us?

Ken Coates

Quacks and crooks

Gill Hubbard and David Miller (editors), *Arguments Against G8*, Pluto Press, 264 pages, paperback ISBN 0745324207, £11.99

David Miller testified to the World Tribunal on Iraq on 'Media wrongs in the war and occupation'. He prefaced his remarks with an invitation to everybody to come to Scotland, to participate in the G8 Alternatives Summit. This was to be 'one of the biggest days of political debate and discussion that Scotland has ever seen'. *Arguments Against G8* is very much an essential primer for those discussions.

Emma Miller sets the tone in her chapter 'The Gang of 8: the good governance roadshow'. She considers what the G8 leaders might be able to do in relation to Africa in the light of 'their domestic governance records, particularly promoting democracy, respecting human rights and observing international law'. The prognosis is not good. What emerges, according to Ms Miller:

> '... is a gang with an impressive criminal profile including corruption, illegal war and crimes against humanity. If we consider the evidence that they are not just quacks, but crooks to boot, their ability to prescribe for Africa is seriously called into question.'

Outspokenness is one of the many strengths of *Arguments Against G8*. Another is its heightened awareness of the extraordinary manipulation, fabrication, and information management that nowadays masquerades as 'news'. Certainly, the editors know all about the 'engineering of consent'. This was very much at the centre of David Miller's previous book for Pluto, *Tell Me Lies: Propaganda and media distortion in the attack on Iraq*. He reminds us in *Arguments* that:

> 'Since 11 September 2001 the Bush and Blair propaganda machines have been overhauled and significantly expanded. The neo-cons have not been alone in their political activism. Their networks tap straight into a very wide range of corporate funded think-tanks and front groups ... But these organisations are not by themselves *the* conspiracy that runs the world. It is not this or that group that is in charge, it is the whole range of organisations working in a community of interest that makes up the global ruling class...They are part of the social movement for global capitalism.'

How much longer must we put up with G8 grandstanding? Is this not a useless assembly which gives affront to the majority of the world's peoples, who are routinely excluded from its deliberations? Is it not a grotesque imposition on the communities whose misfortune it is to be chosen to host such gatherings?

The Metropolitan Police sent 1,500 officers to Scotland to look after the 'eight', their guests and their entourage. Might they not have been better employed in London, where others were marking this annual parade by exploding bombs on the Tube to devastating effect?

Arguments Against G8 is a must-read. Its long list of distinguished contributors includes Noam Chomsky, Salma Yacoob, Caroline Lucas, and Haidi Giuliani, the mother of Carlo who was murdered by policemen four years ago during the G8 Summit in Genoa.

Tony Simpson

We cannot look away

James Kirkup, *No More Hiroshimas,* Spokesman Books, 72 pages, paperback ISBN 0 85124 689 3, £6.99

James Kirkup, who hails from the North East of England, is probably the principal interpreter of Japan to the West and is in this respect the Lafcadio Hearn of our age. His passionate response to Hiroshima is, therefore, both informed and sympathetic as well as widely ranging.

These poems, which also include translations of those by others, have been written over many years. Their spring was his shock in hearing of Hiroshima at a land workers' hostel in Ponteland on the sixth of August 1945. British magazine and book editors, however, were reluctant to publish these poems so he issued them himself in 1983, a collection which was also ignored by reviewers in this country.

There are good poems here and the collection wrestles with one of the central issues of our times. Why should such poems be ignored? One suspects in this rejection a sense of unacknowledged guilt and an insular unconcern with the wider world and with the past, as well as a certain unease with profound seriousness in the arts. There is, in short, a failure of vision, to look both within and without. Their re-publication is both necessary and desirable.

These are not easy poems. They compel us to face the horrors of nuclear warfare and they warn of the much more powerful neutron bomb. They also emphasise that we live in a world of murder, deceit and callous profiteering and that there is a general and cold indifference to the suffering of others such as refugees and of animals. Society is brutal, repressive and intolerant, but we as individuals are also responsible: 'We are all prisoners of one another, / And all our captors are ourselves.' We have, therefore, to see and to reform ourselves, to love each other, to stand against received opinion, and in spite of all to hope and to recall that even in the Second World War 'On both sides / A common brotherhood survived.'

A poet speaks and the message is more powerful for this. There are, for example, 'rainbows' of squid and octopus, a sun 'crudded' in thin snow, and an aged Bertrand Russell with 'the mask of a tragic hawk'. There are, furthermore, the technical bravura of a prosaic obituary in the haiku form, the subversion of a familiar Christmas carol, and biting satire and irony, as in the 'death of sound mind' of a suicide for peace.

In his later years a notable obituarist, Kirkup has in fact throughout his life repeatedly and memorably witnessed to and documented our mortality. The poem sequence 'White shadows' with its insistent, drumming antinomies is surely the canonical response to the white shadow of a man annihilated at Hiroshima. The title poem, moreover, exhibits a characteristic strength, his resolute and unflinching grasp upon reality: with Antaeus and Yeats he keeps his footing firmly on the earth. Hiroshima today is indeed as he depicts it a sad, tawdry, ramshackle and cheaply commercial squalor and emptiness, yet it is here that are preserved the stopped watches, the twisted buttons, and the charred boots of the dead. Amidst the detritus and dereliction of the living there are those also of the dead. As at Auschwitz, it is these pitiful relics which disturb and which we remember. These are 'the memorials we need.'

For Shelley the great gift of poetry is the imagination. Our response to Hiroshima as to Auschwitz and Nanking must be to see and to enter into the experience of others. *Pace* Adorno, there is not today a failure of poetry but of humanity. The task of the poet is to see and to speak without fear or favour and that of the public to read and see. There is here much sane and salutary common sense about nuclear warfare, but it is above all the poet and his vision which matter. He refers in passing to schoolboys abstractedly thumbing pornography with 'second-hand' looks. What he invites us to do here as elsewhere in his work is to see as he does, truly, wholly, and unflinchingly. It is this vision, which earlier readers of these poems lacked, which can free and save us from ourselves. To be healed and whole we must first see what we are and how we behave towards each other.

> 'Questions are hard, but it is worse to remain silent.
> Nor can we afford not to look. We must see all, and say all
> To satisfy the dead who died with such indignity, the shades
> That are watching us, white and speechless. We cannot look away.'

David Burnett

America's Time and Place

Ken Coates, *Empire No More!*, Spokesman Books, 288 pages, hardback ISBN 0 85124 694 X £45, paperback ISBN 085124 700 8 £11.99

We asked Zia Mian for a comment on our recent publication Empire No More! *He sent this analyis of the neo-conservative project for an expanding role for the United States in world affairs.*

In 1997, a group of conservative American politicians, academics and policy brokers announced 'The Project for a New American Century'. The line up reads like a who's who of important players in the Bush administration since 2001. There is vice-president Dick Cheney, defence secretary Donald Rumsfeld, Lewis Libby (Cheney's chief of staff), Paul Wolfowitz, formerly in the defence department and newly appointed president of the World Bank, and Zalmay Khalilzad (who has served until recently as the ambassador to Afghanistan and is now the ambassador to Iraq). It also includes Jeb Bush, president Bush's brother.

The Project for a New American Century is focused on the concern that 'American foreign and defence policy is adrift'. They worry that the US may not have what they describe as the 'resolve to shape a new century favourable to American principles and interests'. They seem disappointed in the willingness of Americans to take up the burden of America's role in the world. The Project's goal, they say, is to 'make the case and rally support for American global leadership'.

Their name and vision clearly echo Henry Luce's famous 1941 manifesto 'The American Century' in *Life* magazine. Luce starts his essay by observing that 'We Americans are unhappy. We are not happy with America. We are not happy about ourselves in relation to America. We are nervous – or gloomy or apathetic.' The rest of the essay can be read as an argument as to why Americans should make a decision to find some thing that will, as he says, 'inspire us to live and work and fight with vigour and enthusiasm'. If they can do this, Luce says, then Americans can 'create the first great American century'.

According to Luce, there was a war that was waiting to be fought. It was not just the Second World War, but a much larger struggle. This was the war that

Americans had been evading for decades. He wrote:

> 'The fundamental trouble with Americans has been, and is, that whereas their nation became in the 20th century the most powerful and the most vital nation in the world, nevertheless Americans were unable to accommodate themselves spiritually and practically to that fact. Hence they have failed to play their part as a world power – a failure which has had disastrous consequences for themselves and for all mankind. And the cure is this: to accept wholeheartedly our duty and our opportunity as the most powerful and vital nation in the world and in consequence to exert upon the world the full impact of our influence, for such purposes as we see fit and by such means as we see fit.'

Luce was calling on America to embrace a role as a global empire. There are few who would disagree that after the Second World War the United States did just what Luce proposed. It took the opportunity that was available and exerted on the world all the influence it could for the purposes and with all the means that its leaders saw fit. In 2002, president Bush declared 'Today, the US enjoys a position of unparalleled military strength and great economic and political influence'. But looking back over these 60 years or so and looking around the world and America now, it is clear that American 'global leadership' has proven to be a short-lived and difficult period of global domination and the whole idea is in crisis again.

In the aftermath of the Second World War, the United States used all kinds of power in its effort to exert influence. One study that tried to list the US use of its armed forces 'as part of a deliberate attempt by the national authorities to influence, or to be prepared to influence, specific behaviour of individuals in another nation without engaging in a continuing contest of violence' cites 215 incidents between 1946 and 1975. The list excludes actual wars. A 1998 study looked at policy in the post-Cold War period and observed that 'Unencumbered by Cold War fears of sparking confrontation with the powerful Soviet Union, American policy-makers turned frequently to threats and the use of force'. It examined eight major cases of US threats and use of force in that period and concluded 'The US sometimes succeeded in these ventures and sometimes failed. Success rarely came easily, however; more often, the US had to go to great lengths to persuade adversaries to yield to its will.' Even without a superpower enemy, America was not prevailing easily.

The United States at the end of the Second World War also created new international institutions, including the United Nations. It has run into problems with this as well. At the founding conference in San Francisco in 1945, 50 nations met to draw up the Charter. There were disagreements between Britain, the Soviet Union, and the United States on one side and the less powerful nations on the other, with the major powers insisting that the Charter give them power to veto actions by the Security Council. A history of the debate and the UN veto records that 'At one point during the conference,... several delegations of smaller nations became somewhat unruly in their opposition to the veto', whereupon one of the US delegates told them that 'they could go home from San Francisco if they wished and report that they had defeated the veto but they could also report that they had torn up the Charter.'

The United States got its way. But here, too, success was not to last or to come easily. In the first flush of the post-Cold War world, secretary of state Madeleine Albright claimed that 'the UN is a tool of American foreign policy'. A few years later, in trying to get UN support for the use of force against Iraq, president Bush found himself with no option but to threaten its very existence, declaring to the UN General Assembly 'Will the United Nations serve the purpose of its founding, or will it be irrelevant?' Nonetheless, the threat was ignored and, despite US bullying and bribes, the overwhelming majority of Security Council members refused to support the US resolution authorising an attack on Iraq.

It is not just governments. People around the world have been responding. A January 2005 Pew study on global opinion, based on their polling in recent years in 44 countries, reported that 'the rest of the world has become deeply suspicious of US motives and openly sceptical about its word'. It observed that 'Anti-Americanism is deeper and broader now than at any time in modern history. It is most acute in the Muslim world but it spans the globe – from Europe to Asia, from South America to Africa.' This includes people in countries that have been close US allies for over 50 years.

The Pew survey found that these opinions were enduring, noting that 'this new hardening of attitudes amounts to something much larger than a thumbs down on the current occupant of the White House'. Pew reported that 'at the heart of the decline in world opinion about America is the perception that the United States acts internationally without taking into account the interests of other nations'. A December 2004 public opinion poll in 23 countries found that in 20 of these countries a majority of citizens believed it would be better for Europe to become more influential than the United States in world affairs.

Nowhere is the decline in the 'global leadership' of the United States more evident than in its occupation of Iraq. The much vaunted 'coalition of the willing' that the Bush administration claimed to have built in 2003 for the invasion of Iraq has all but collapsed. Thirteen countries have already withdrawn their forces. Italy, Poland, and Ukraine have all recently announced they will pull their troops out; these are the fourth, fifth and sixth largest contingents of foreign troops there. The countries that will soon be left, apart from United States and the United Kingdom, are Albania, Armenia, Azerbaijan, Bulgaria, Czech Republic, El Salvador, Estonia, Georgia, Kazakhstan, Latvia, Lithuania, Macedonia, Mongolia, Romania, Slovakia, South Korea, Japan, Denmark and Australia.

President Bush's leadership at home is in deep trouble too. The *Washington Post* noted that his election victory in 2004 was far from the mandate he claimed it to be. He received 50.7 per cent of the popular vote, while John Kerry managed to get 48.2 per cent. The last time a president was re-elected with such a small margin was almost two hundred years ago, in the early 1800s. President Bush now has the lowest approval rating of any president at this point in his second term, according to polls going back to the Second World War.

Domestic US opinion is now uneasy about the war. United for Peace and

Justice, a national network of anti-war groups, counted 583 towns and cities around the country that were planning events to mark the second anniversary of the war. This is up from 319 such events last year. In the state of Vermont, in a day of coordinated town meetings, 49 out of 57 communities approved resolutions calling for the withdrawal of US troops from Iraq. A March *Washington Post-ABC News* poll found that 53 per cent of Americans feel the war was not worth fighting, 57 per cent say they disapprove of Bush's handling of Iraq, and 70 per cent think the number of US casualties is an unacceptable price to have paid.

It is not just the Iraq war. The American public seems to be telling pollsters that they do not support a 'global leadership' role for their country. Only about eight per cent supported a hegemonic role for the United States, as the 'pre-eminent world leader in solving international problems'. There was little difference between Republicans and Democrats. The overwhelming majority agreed that 'The United States should do its share in efforts to solve international problems together with other countries'. Asked the same question another way: 'Do you think that the United States has the responsibility to play the role of "world policeman"', they gave the same answer – overwhelming majorities, over 70 per cent were opposed. Even larger majorities criticised existing policy, by saying that 'The United States is playing the role of world policeman more than it should be'.

There is more than just rejection of the idea of global domination. There is widespread support among the American public for the United States submitting to international institutions and the will of the international community. A poll in March 2005 found that 57 per cent of Americans believed that the United States should not have an absolute veto at the United Nations, and agreed that if a decision was supported by all the other members, no one member, not even the United States, should be able to veto it. Almost 60 per cent of Americans believed that the United Nations should become 'significantly more powerful in worlds affairs'. Asked whether, 'when dealing with international problems, the United States should be more willing to make decisions within the United Nations even if this means that the US will sometimes have to go along with a policy that is not its first choice,' 75 per cent of those who described themselves as Democrats said that it should as did 50 per cent of Republicans.

Majorities also agree that the United States should join the International Criminal Court, even if that meant US troops possibly being brought to trial there; sign the Kyoto Climate Change Treaty; ratify the Comprehensive Nuclear Test Ban Treaty, and the convention banning landmines. There was even widespread public support for the United States accepting and being bound by adverse decisions from the World Trade Organisation.

Henry Luce would be deeply disappointed. It seems that the majority of Americans remain, as he put it, 'unable to accommodate themselves spiritually and practically' to empire. If the people have their way, the American century may turn out to be much shorter that he or his successors at the Project for a New American Century could ever have imagined.

Zia Mian

Russell unchained

Bertrand Russell, *What I Believe*, Routledge Classics, 48 pages, ISBN 0415325099 £7.99

Bertrand Russell's short essay has now appeared in a handsome new format as part of Routledge's series of Classics.

The essay was first published as a contribution to a series of booklets which included the more famous *Icarus* by Russell, which was a response to J. B. S. Haldane's tract, *Daedalus*. Haldane was full of optimism about the prospects of a scientific world. Russell, ever agnostic, argued that science gave Icarus the power of flight, but not the intelligence to fly wisely.

This little book appears with a sympathetic and balanced preface by Alan Ryan, but close examination shows that the cover illustrates a dark process of enchainment. Are these the mind-forged manacles of man? Or do they represent the freedom that will attend the reader once he has gone beyond them?

KC

Arms spending dwarfs aid

SIPRI Yearbook 2005: Armaments, Disarmament and International Security, Oxford University Press, 840 pages, ISBN 0-19-928401-6 and 978-0-19-928401-6, £80

The Stockholm International Peace Research Institute (SIPRI) has reported its findings for global military expenditure in 2004. It increased to $975 billion at 2003 prices ($1,035 billion at current prices). This is equivalent to $162 per capita worldwide, and represents a 6% rise in real terms over the three years from 2002. It is more than 14 times greater than world spending on overseas aid in 2003 (no figures are available yet for aid in 2004).

The United States accounted for 47% of world military expenditure in 2004, spending $455 billion (at 2003 prices). In other words, the US spent more than six times as much on its military in 2004 than the whole world spent on aid for the world's poorest in 2003. Of the $455 billion, approximately $238 billion was raised almost exclusively for military operations in Afghanistan and Iraq. The bills for US military operations in Iraq and Afghanistan in 2004 were greater than the military expenditure of the entire developing world (Africa, Latin America, the Middle East, Asia except Japan but including China) for the year.

In 2003, the United Kingdom was the third largest military spender; in 2004, it had risen to second place, spending $47.4 billion (at 2003 prices — US dollars used to aid comparisons). This is roughly equivalent to the additional amount of aid spending worldwide that the World Bank estimates is required to achieve the United Nations Millennium Development Goals ($40-70 billion per annum to 2015).

The highest per capita spending on arms of any country was by Israel, at $1,627 for every citizen in 2004 (at 2003 prices). The United States was close behind at $1,533. The UK figure was $798.

David Gee

Human rights and the UN

Luckshan Abeysuriya, *The UN Commission on Human Rights has failed the international human rights movement*, 18 pages. ISBN 0953 183912. £3. Available from LA Accounting Services, 'Mallaig', The Crescent, Grange Over Sands, Cumbria LA11 6AW.

The author has given us a very useful succinct history of the United Nations Commission on Human Rights (UNCHR) from its foundation in 1948 under the Universal Declaration of Human Rights until the present day.

Abeysuriya traces the development of UNCHR from a body consisting of only 18 member states, through its expansion from 1967 onwards, to today's membership of 53 countries. He shows how this expansion, by bringing in African, Asian and South American states, widened enormously the scope for focus on human rights from its early Cold War preoccupation to many more areas of concern to the non-aligned movement.

The pamphlet rightly stresses the importance over the last decade or so of Non-Governmental Organisations in influencing the work of the Commission, especially over such achievements as the UN Convention on Torture. (As a board member till recently of Amnesty International, Luckshan Abeysuriya is in a good position to recognise the influence of that organisation on this positive outcome).

But while the Commission has been much more effective as a forum, the author judges that its achievements as an 'actor' have been disappointingly few. The author believes strongly that a reformed UNCHR could have a vital role in the promotion of human rights, but is sceptical whether reform proposals presently on the table can help overcome the stalemate of competing national interests, especially in a world obsessed with terrorism and preoccupied with 'draconian emergency legislation'.

Ken Fleet

New Left Review

In recent issues:

Susan Watkins: Europe's political landscape after the French and Dutch votes
Jean Baudrillard discusses the meaning of the 'Non'
Richard Gott on Tony Blair and the death of the Labour Party
Giovanni Arrighi's landmark engagement with Harvey's *New Imperialism*
Wang Chaohua examines national consciousness in Taiwan
John Newsinger on British atrocities in Kenya
Mustafa Barghouti reflects on the Palestinian struggle
Gopal Balakrishnan on Machiavelli's parables of innovation
Perry Anderson: Rawls, Habermas and Bobbio in an age of serial war
Lu Xinyu analyses China's new documentary cinema
Lucio Magri discusses the closure of Italy's leading Left monthly
Pascale Casanova: power and subversion in the World Republic of Letters

An annual subscription, which costs £32, includes free access to NLR's Digital Archive, 1960–2005, and a free Verso book.

Visit our website to read sample articles and subscribe online:

www.newleftreview.org